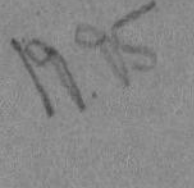
19.95

D1573134

The American Clock

1725-1865

The American Clock
1725-1865

The Mabel Brady Garvan and Other Collections at Yale University

Essay and Technical Notes by EDWIN A. BATTISON

Commentary by PATRICIA E. KANE

Foreword by CHARLES F. MONTGOMERY

Introduction by DEREK DE SOLLA PRICE

New York Graphic Society Limited • Greenwich, Connecticut

International Standard Book Number
0-8212-0493-9
Library of Congress Catalog Card Number
72-93856

First published 1973 by New York Graphic Society Ltd., 140 Greenwich Ave., Greenwich, Conn., 06830
First Printing 1973
Second Printing 1974

Designed by Ray Ripper

Manufactured in the U.S.A.

This book is dedicated to

MABEL BRADY GARVAN

in whose honor many of the clocks here catalogued were given to Yale

and to the memory of her husband

FRANCIS P. GARVAN '97

who gave his superlative collection of American art to Yale

foreword

Forty-one of the clocks described and illustrated in this book were a part of Francis P. Garvan's magnificent gift of American arts to Yale University in honor of his wife, Mabel Brady Garvan, in 1930. Later, before his death in 1937, Mr. Garvan, B.A. 1897, gave three more clocks. For the most part, the clocks of the Garvan gift were the tall clocks so highly prized by eighteenth-century Americans.

Following Mr. Garvan's lead, tall clocks were given to Yale by Mrs. Clark McIlwaine of West Hartford and Washington, D.C., in 1946; by Charles Bain Hoyt in 1950; by Josephine Thacher of New Haven in 1954; and by Nathalie Penrose Swetland of Hartford and Coventry, Connecticut, in memory of William Rex Penrose, in 1966. A fine tall clock made by Benjamin Rittenhouse came to Yale through the bequest of Walter B. Sheppard, B.A. 1887, of Denver, in 1950. In 1954 Charles Stetson, B.A. 1900, of Boston, bequeathed two Aaron Willard shelf clocks to his University. Among the three clocks (two shelf and one tall clock) bequeathed to Yale in 1962 by Miss Olive L. Dann of New Haven, the Eli Terry pillar and scroll clock was a particularly important addition, representing as it does a whole new era in the American clockmaking industry.

At the time of Francis Garvan's gift to Yale in 1930, many of his clocks were on loan to historic houses up and down the Atlantic seaboard, where they had been seen and admired for twenty years or more. However, as plans developed in the late 1950's for the publication of the Garvan and Related Collections of American Arts at Yale it was determined to bring all of the collections scattered about the country back to New Haven for study, research, and restoration. This task was undertaken by Meyric Rogers, who, after a distinguished career as Curator of American Decorative Arts at the Art Institute of Chicago, was named Curator of the Garvan and Related Collections in 1958, a position he held until 1964. Following his appointment, Mr. Rogers brought together in the Garvan Furniture Study—located in the basement of the Yale University Press building—some seven hundred pieces of furniture, including more than fifty clocks. There, preliminary cataloguing and the first steps toward publication were begun about 1960.

In 1962 Willard I. Andrews, then Chairman of the Exhibitions Committee and Vice-President of the National Association of Watch and Clock Collectors, wrote Yale for information about its collection of clocks, which he wished to include in his survey of clock collections "open to public view." Almost immediately thereafter he began to prod Mr. Rogers and his assistant, John T. Kirk, to put the clocks in running order and to prepare information about them for early publication instead of delaying their appearance until Volume Three of the projected furniture catalogue. Mr. Andrews persevered, and soon after Jules Prown's appointment as Curator in 1964 to succeed Mr. Rogers, Mr. Andrews came to New Haven and again expressed strong interest in the restoration of the clock movements. In response to Mr. Prown's explanation of the delay—Yale's lack of funds and the need to catalogue the movements as well as restore them—Mr. Andrews made arrangements through Nelson Booth, a Yale alumnus, for three New Hampshire clock collectors, Edwin B. Burt, Charles S. Parsons, and Frederick M. Selchow, to come to New Haven for a preliminary survey of the collection in October of 1966, at which time they entered basic information about each clock on an excellent data sheet prepared by Mr. Parsons.

The following September (1967), Edwin A. Battison of the Smithsonian Institution was engaged by Mr. Prown to prepare descriptions and catalogue notes on the movements. Subsequently, in December 1967, Moussa Domit, Registrar of the Yale University Art Gallery, arranged to have fifty-two clock movements taken to the Museum of History and Technology, the Smithsonian Institution, for restoration. There, thanks to the good offices of Peter Welsh and Robert Multhauf, space was provided for study and the necessary cleaning and restoration, which were undertaken under Mr. Battison's supervision by Ronald D. Sweetland, an independent clock restorer of Hyattsville, Maryland. Just at this time in response to Mr. Prown's plea came a grant from the National Association of Watch and Clock Collectors of $2500 in support of publication of the clocks.

Patricia E. Kane, a graduate of the Winterthur Program of Early American Culture, was named Assistant Curator of the Garvan Collection in July 1968. During that summer, with the assistance of Roger Howlett, Curatorial Assistant, and Elton Weyland Hall, a 1968 graduate of the Winterthur Program, she diligently studied and prepared condition reports for each clock case. Soon thereafter Charles Uht, New York photographer, began to make the beautiful photographs with which this book is illustrated—the movements having been returned from Washington and reunited with their cases.

After Mr. Prown's appointment as Director of the Mellon Center in 1968, general supervision of the project was shifted to Theodore E. Stebbins, Jr., Associate Curator of the Garvan and Related Collections. During the spring of 1969 he invited Mr. Prown and the writer to meet on several occasions to discuss content and format of the furniture catalogue with Miss Kane. At that time it was tentatively decided to publish the clocks as a separate book and Miss Kane began to write commentary for each clock case.

During 1971 and 1972 the manuscript was brought to completion with the coordination of the information on movements and cases and the preparation of a general bibliography and glossary by Miss Kane.

Tribute should be paid to all of the above individuals for their contributions to this catalogue, and in particular to the National Association of Watch and Clock Collectors. We are also grateful to: Edward La Fond, Jr., who read the manuscript and made helpful suggestions; Fernande Ross, editor (1966-69) of the Garvan furniture catalogue, who did much of the preliminary work; Gillian Farmer, who typed the manuscript, and especially Marion Sandquist, who prepared the last several drafts; Elizabeth Smith, who under Mr. Prown's supervision prepared a bibliography for each clock; and to E. Irving Blomstrann, Joseph Szaszfai, and William C. Howze, who made additional photographs for the catalogue.

Special thanks are owed to Derek J. de Solla Price, Avalon Professor of the History of Science, for his introduction on changing attitudes toward clocks and clockmaking through the ages.

From the preliminary work sheets prepared by Messrs Burt, Parsons, and Selchow and the initial study of the cases by Meyric Rogers and John Kirk, to the final manuscript, there were many stages of development, but ultimately the final version has been clearly the responsibility and work of Patricia E. Kane and Edwin A. Battison.

Throughout the ten years this publication has been under way Mrs. Francis P. Garvan has been patient. Year after year she has given encouragement and financial support. We thank her warmly. We hope that she will be pleased when she sees the final product—America's handsomest, best-illustrated and most detailed American clock book.

Charles F. Montgomery

New Haven, January 1973

contents

introduction

A Cultural History of Clocks

Derek de Solla Price

It is well known that timekeepers, such as sundials of all sorts, existed long before the birth of the clock, but few people realize that gear-wheeled clockwork was used centuries before it was adapted to the clock as timekeeper. Indeed, the long and seemingly paradoxical history of clocks must be known if one is to understand the enormous fascination they have had, the craftsmanship and ingenuity that were lavished on them, and the mass market that developed for them. Moreover, this history is closely associated with many of the roots of the Industrial Revolution and the age of the computer, as well as with the characteristics of Yankee ingenuity that shaped the destiny of America. Such history surely must be ascribed to something more forceful than curiosity or the need to know the correct time; the cultural history of clocks involves very much more than the story of timekeeping.

Clockwork, the use of trains of toothed wheels, begins—virtually in its modern form—in the classical period of Greek civilization. Long before this, man had evolved the habit and the techniques of modeling the world about him and its forces in order to comprehend and control them. From the Lascaux cave paintings to the idols and "ritual objects" of all the ancient cultures we have much evidence of these efforts. With the Greeks, philosophical inquiry and scientific understanding reached a new level; in two directions in particular, astronomy and medicine, the advances were so considerable as to change the very nature of these models of the universe, the understanding they brought, and the control that they imparted.

Astronomy and medicine were in many ways the most vital sciences, since they comprehended the two halves of creation, the inanimate and the animate world. For the animate world of medicine the metaphor of creation was that of the *pneuma* (from which the term "pneumatic" derives), a conceptual model in which fluids, airy and liquid, are supposed to be piped through the body, and by their various motions and reactions cause all change and movement, health and disease.

For the inanimate world of astronomy it was natural to see the sun and moon, the planets and the stars, turned with great regularity as by wheels, each at its proper speed. Quite early in the Greek age models of the universe were embodied by philosophers in a convention of actual wheels, cut in metal and made to turn at the appropriate rates by gear teeth. The toothed wheel seems to have been devised for this, rather than for any workaday machine. At all events, we know that Archimedes made such a mechanical planetarium, and we know that later models were even turned automatically by water power instead of by a handle, such as probably turned the original. We have evidence that several of these planetarium-type devices were made, and fragments of a very complicated specimen from the first century B.C., containing differential gearing and more than thirty gear-wheels, were recovered from a sunken treasure ship in 1901, in the first attempt at underwater archaeology.

Making models of animate beings also became a tradition, for which we have textual evidence in the writings of Heron of Alexandria (second century A.D.), who devised an automaton theater with birds that flapped their wings and whistled, and with many other self-propelled puppet figures. Although his automata were powered by water and by air pressure, in illustration of the *pneuma*, Heron's writings indicate that he was also interested in the simple uses of gear-wheels. It used to be fashionable to decry these models of creation as mere toys and trickery, but it is perhaps more realistic to see them as scientific models, as important for their time as mathematical models have been more recently in the growth of science.

The Greek tradition of model making was never lost; it passed to the scientists and craftsmen of Islam, where it was elaborated and improved, and from Islam was directly transmitted to medieval Europe. In the Middle Ages, in the East and West, there was considerable activity in the building and improvement of astronomical models of all sorts, and from these there gradually evolved the fine craft of the scientific instrument maker, which led to the injection of experimental techniques into the Scientific Revolution.

Some time in the twelfth century a similar and equally ancient line of model making, using astronomical models powered by waterwheels and regulated by tripping levers, was transmitted to the West from China, presumably with the help of returning Crusaders. A link is missing in our historical evidence, but it seems that this led to the creation, quite anonymously, of the modern form of mechanical clock. In effect, the astronomical model was now powered by a weight drive instead of by water, and it was regulated by a rocking device similar to that which had been used in the automata for bell ringing.

Yet at this time the clock was still primarily an astronomical model rather than a timekeeper. Though we know of the existence of several clocks in the thirteenth and earlier fourteenth century, the first one of which we have full details is that built by Giovanni de Dondi in Padua in 1364, and that one was covered with complicated dials showing every planet and the calendar, and only incidentally did it simulate the daily motion of the sun and actually tell time.

Later in the Middle Ages the great cathedral clocks, all of them highly astronomical, swept over Europe in a great orgy of clockwork made to the glory of God. Their purpose was not at first to tell the time or the duration of the sermon, nor indeed to herald the appropriate time for prayers; they were made to exemplify and model God's creation through understanding. The timing of prayer, however, may have been quite important for the development of the clock as a timer, for the ritual observance of prayer times to the cry of the muezzin in Islam became a principal externalization of the Moslem faith, and similarly in later Christian Europe canonical observances of the monastic rule required the timekeeper. It is perhaps worthy of note that the great cathedral clocks of the Middle Ages commonly have not only the astronomical model but also the animate model, the jackwork of little figures in procession, the mannikins that ring bells and blow trumpets, and the golden cock that crows at the dawn. In fact, the chimes of the modern clock, the moon dial and calendar that occur on so many clocks in Yale's collection, and the cuckoo of the Black Forest clock are all much older than the mechanical clock tradition itself.

Perhaps more important than the clocks themselves was the evolution begun during the Middle Ages, and developed much further in the Renaissance and Reformation, of the rather specialized class of ingenious craftsmen who built clocks, and later also watches. With the organization of the trade guilds, first in Germany and then all over Europe, the clockmakers rose to prominence and acted as a reservoir of skill in fine-metalwork and ingenious mechanical devices. The public's fascination with model universes and with concrete examples of mechanistic understanding expanded, becoming a fascination with scientific gadgetry and experimental science. Almost from the beginning of experimental science, it was the clockmakers who had the competence to make scientific instruments. The association continued practically to modern times; certainly through the eighteenth century it was very common for the clockmakers to be the makers, the dealers, and the promulgators of surveying instruments, navigation aids, barometers, optical instruments, and all other scientific devices. As the use of scientific instruments became more widespread there was, of course, some tendency for this trade to separate from that of the clockmakers, but the central force of ingenuity still resided in skilled fine-metalworkers, and the fascination with their products remained that powerful force that led the Greeks to automata and the medieval world to the astronomical cathedral clocks.

One of the prime forces in the Industrial Revolution that began in the eighteenth century and stretched through the nineteenth was this same combination of skill in the mechanism and fascination with it. Though the millwright and the blacksmith also intervened in clockmaking with their technological crafts (in fact among the blacksmiths there were ingenious craftsmen who made the iron public clocks that adorned so many churches), it is the clockmaker who led, and the clock that was the archetypal machine of the burgeoning of the Industrial Revolution. The backroom inventor of complicated machinery, so typical of the nineteenth century, was driven by the old fascination as much as by material hopes of a successful and utilitarian creation that would generate a market and bring him profit.

Though the old line remained dominant through the period, it is quite clear that the impact of the Scientific and Industrial Revolutions brought radical changes in clockmaking. The principal changes came from the growth in the basic scientific and technical skills and the greater prevalence of machinery, factors that made the clock at the same time less special in its fascination and function and much more readily available. The clock became much more accurate and reliable, much more valuable scientifically, much more widespread in its social impact; it changed gradually from an object of wonder, value, ingenuity, and craft skill, to one of utility, general furnishing, and trade manufacture. The clockmakers, however, though moving with the changes, cannot be understood without reference to that older tradition that continued to make the social function of the clock different from that of the new machinery and new styles of furniture.

In many histories of the clock one points to the scientific changes in the seventeenth century, particularly the introduction of the pendulum around 1670, as the chief force in the metamorphosis of the clock. The development of the pendulum led to the design of the anchor escapement to replace the old, and allegedly unreliable, verge that oscillated a foliot, or crown wheel. True, the pendulum is neatly and mathematically isochronous, but in the beginning clockmakers were overly impressed with this, designing special cycloidal cheeks that turned out to be an unwelcome and avoidable refinement. Furthermore, the old style escapement, though rough in household clocks (such as that illustrated in Figs. 1, 2), was all that was required for them; when more was needed, it would be supplied—for example, in the 1580's, when Tycho Brahe demanded high accuracy for his observatory, Justus Bürgi made a double cross-beating verge escapement that probably exceeded the early pendulum clocks in accuracy. The pendulum was fascinating because it worked on the principles of the newly triumphant Newtonian astronomy. It did, however, mean a new approach to clocks and a basic change in shape to accommodate its length. By 1700 the tall case clock had become dominant, and by the 1720's it was refined by elegant application of mercury or gridiron pendulums so that the high-accuracy clock became possible. The technique generated a market, and a style would develop in the nineteenth century of stripping the clock of all nonessentials and belligerently asserting that its function was high accuracy. These "regulator" clocks became popular, not only in the observatories where they belonged, but also in men's clubs and other gathering places where one could use them for setting less reliable watches and clocks before the advent of the radio and telephone time signals. Yale University had such a clock in its observatory, and for some time it was used to supply the New Haven Railroad and the local telegraphic service with the correct time (Figs. 3-6, on pages 14 and 15).

The development of the tall case clock (not called a "grandfather" clock till 1876, when Henry Clay Work inadvertently popularized the name through his song) and the increased market for clocks and scientific instruments had a positive effect: the number of mass workshops increased and these established virtually line manufacture of semi-standardized wheels that were much better made and more carefully balanced and pivoted—better designed, in short—than clockwork ever had been before. The wall clock and shelf clock developed with increased familiarity with and confidence in the use of short pendulums that beat faster than once per second. Their popularity was furthered in England

Fig. 1

Fig. 2

by the parliamentary acts of 1797–98, which attempted to tax the rising new industry. Just as window taxes changed architectural styles, so taxes on individual clocks produced a resurgence of the public clock; the "Act of Parliament clocks" on tavern walls became familiar, and when the tax subsided they acted as an impetus to the production of domestic wall and shelf clocks.

Yankee ingenuity, a major force in the history of the United States, can be identified with the clockmakers, whose social reactions differed widely from their counterparts in Europe. In the earliest days the makers of clocks were in effect merely transplanted Europeans as far as their craft and techniques were concerned. The orreries and clocks of David Rittenhouse were exactly in the tradition that runs from the Greek automata to the de Dondi clock and the orreries of Rittenhouse's contemporaries in London and Paris; Benjamin Franklin's concern for clock design is paralleled by that of many members of the Royal Society in London. The minor craftsmen who came after Rittenhouse and Franklin, however, entered a new world, with different materials, different needs, and a break in the continuity of apprenticeship. What developed was the very essence of Yankee ingenuity. Techniques were borrowed from the millwright and wheelwright rather than from the fine-metalworker; the clock as a piece of furniture was molded by the new sort of peddler who could sell it, and by the settler moving to the frontier who could buy it as an almost symbolic adornment to indicate the new stability and prosperity of a new home. Helped by trade embargoes and war restrictions, the native trade and skill grew along lines not matched in Europe and led to the age of Eli Terry and Simon Willard, to fresh ingenuity in design and manufacture.

With the coming of the railroad and the telegraph and the growth of big cities, the clock became functional in a new way that is now so universal that it is difficult to think back to that earlier age. Time became national and universal, an orderer of daily life and appointments and schedules, and the clock became a utilitarian device only tinged by its former glory. □

◁ **Figs. 1, 2**
Iron chamber clock with verge and foliot escapement, probably Swiss, early sixteenth century, now in the collection of Berkeley College, Yale University. Such simple clocks, descended from the astronomical masterpieces, are a direct continuation of the medieval tradition of prependulum clockwork. They needed daily regulation by a sundial and probably annual mechanical care, but were tolerably reliable and accurate with such care and could ring out the hours day and night for the use of a large and affluent household.

Fig. 3

Fig. 4

Fig. 5

Fig. 6

Figs. 3-6

Tall case regulator clock by Henry Appleton, London (ca. 1840), now in the Yale Collection of Historic Scientific Instruments. This clock was formerly the standard clock of the Yale Astronomical Observatory and for a brief period was used to supply accurate time signals to the New Haven Railroad. As the casing indicates, such clocks also served a more domestic purpose, being commonly used in gathering places and clubs, where they provided standard time for setting pocket watches. The temperature-compensated mercury pendulum regulates a movement stripped to its minimum of complication (Fig. 6), made with great precision and totally enclosed as a protection against dust (Fig. 5). The characteristic special dial (Fig. 4) has a centrally mounted minute hand, a seconds dial above driven directly from the escapement wheel, and a twenty-four-hour dial below. The pronounced simplicity of the works and dial is a foretaste of the emphasis on functionalism in the clock in the later nineteenth century, when it is seen as a precision timekeeper, stripped of ornamentation and incidentals.

essay

The Development of American Clocks and Clockmaking

Edwin A. Battison

An antique clock is seen differently by different people. To some it may be just a piece of furniture, to some a work of art, to others a convenience, to a few a document of craft techniques. More than once I have heard clocks described as having personalities, as being companionable. One clock may be all these things. So it is with those of the Garvan Collection, one of the great collections of American clocks.

In the early colonies the first clocks were imported, most of them unsophisticated wall clocks with open weights, reflecting the modest economic status of the colonists. When clockmaking did begin in the new land, it at first closely reflected the styles and techniques of Europe. The pendulum was introduced there in the last third of the seventeenth century and brought important changes in clock design. Some of the older clocks were converted at that time to pendulum control, sometimes with the addition of the newly practical minute hand; other features, such as dial and bell, remained unchanged. The most conspicuous change came with the development of the cased clock, the type that housed movement and pendulum in an impressive tall case.

The earliest American clockmakers had been trained in Europe, chiefly in Britain, and in the colonies they continued to make clocks in their original manner, especially the tall (or long case, or "grandfather") clock. But they found conditions somewhat different in America, particularly if they had settled inland or in areas outside the mainstream of trade: for one thing, they had to integrate their work with that of the supporting craftsmen available—engravers, dial painters, and cabinetmakers with varying degrees of skill. As a result they were forced to modify or simplify their European models, to innovate and improvise. Then a new generation of apprentices, American-trained, further Americanized the product. The greatest innovators may have been the self-taught, or those who came to clockmaking from other branches of the mechanical arts. These men often began in a humble way; having grasped the essential principles of the mechanism, they expressed them freely, being less bound by traditional methods than the conventionally trained clockmakers.

Thus by the mid-eighteenth century one native school of clockmaking developed: local craftsmen built the movement in the medium most familiar to them, wood, readily available in the agricultural and forest economy of colonial America. The early wooden clocks of Connecticut are representative of the school (for example the works of Benjamin and Timothy Cheney of East Hartford), but it is not easy to say who originated the type or to identify the various practitioners. In spirit, their work may be likened to the unsophisticated folk craft of the early Black Forest clockmakers.

American clockmakers—or more likely their customers—were conservative and held closely to the familiar appearance of the European-style tall clock until the early nineteenth century. Within these rather rigid conventions of appearance are found clocks with both metal and wooden movements, clocks ranging from the simplest one-hand timepiece to complex examples with minute and second hands, with striking mechanisms, calendar dials and dials showing the phases of the moon. The absence or presence of these features is far more an expression of the customer's taste than of the maker's ability or sophistication. The cabinet is usually indicative of whether the movement was cased in one of the fashionable centers or had been taken to a frontier area before being cased. Many of the early machine-made grandfather clocks distributed by peddlers received "coffin-makers' cases"—so named because the workmanship betrayed limited ability, all that was required to make such a simple and expendable item as a coffin.

By the closing years of the eighteenth century the impact of the Industrial Revolution was felt at all levels in the clock business. The manufacture of brass clocks was simplified by the appearance of semifinished parts, including dials and hands, usually imported. About the same time, wooden clocks began to be made in quantity by the use of power-driven machinery. These innovations offered convenience as well as opportunity for profit, and they were already gaining acceptance when new factors made the outlook still more promising. The Jefferson Embargo of December 1807 and the Non-Intercourse Act of 1809 had the effect of protective tariffs, and with the War of 1812, which further disrupted foreign trade, they provided a great spur to domestic industry. All kinds of clockmaking flourished during this period, as demand exceeded supply. Makers producing clocks made of conventional materials—brass, iron, and steel—found these in short supply and consequently expensive.

It was a situation reminiscent of that prevailing during and just after the Revolution, when the Willards in Massachusetts introduced shelf clocks that were economical of metal and, because of their small size, could be made faster and sold at a lower price than the conventional tall clocks. Benjamin Willard, the first Willard clockmaker and brother of the famous Simon, picked up clockmaking about 1764 from Benjamin Cheney of Hartford, Connecticut—Cheney, ironically, was a leading maker of wooden clocks. With this background, Benjamin Willard, or his brothers Simon and Aaron, who learned from him, might have developed the kind of scaled-down wooden clock that Eli Terry created later. However, the Willards and those around them were not oriented toward new or high-quantity production techniques, although they introduced many new forms, some showing marked French influence. Most durable of the line was the banjo clock patented by Simon Willard in 1802.

But aggressive as the Willards were, they were not destined to alter radically the course of clockmaking because they were not sufficiently free of traditional concepts. The cutting off of imports, which was a hindrance to them and other clockmakers in the old tradition, was a boon to those making the humbler wooden clocks, who enjoyed an unlimited supply of native raw materials. The making of wooden components by power-driven machinery instead of by highly skilled labor was already established, and now this cost-reducing practice was widely extended. Wooden clockmaking came to be recognized as a means to acquiring riches, and it therefore attracted many practitioners of limited abilities who were merely businessmen and producers, rather than inventive craftsmen. Eventually this led to intense competition and the inevitable price cutting, accompanied by a decline in the quality of workmanship.

Faced with this difficult situation, some of the more imaginative and astute practitioners brought out new designs, such as the eight-day movement for the tall clock. One man of unusual vision and business sense proved to be the leading innovator, Eli Terry, who developed a radically new clock. Troubled by the intense competition and lowered standards in tall clock manufacture, he sold his business in 1810 and ostensibly retired. Using his new leisure, he developed the shelf clock, patented in 1816. This clock was better adapted than the tall clock to the small but still gracious homes being built in great numbers in the settled East, as well as to the modest homes of the advancing frontier. The case of the shelf clock was rich-looking, but it could be made at the factory—thus adding to the profit made by the change in raw materials—and its small size made it easier to transport.

The shelf clock was a more-than-successful rival to the other distinctively American clock, the brass-works banjo clock by Simon Willard, still hand-made and expensive. Terry's clock was such a radical departure that extensive production runs of several models were made before the basic ideas were expressed in a form ideally adapted to economical mass production and reliable performance. The clock was introduced during the period of depressed business conditions that followed the peace of 1816, when most of the infant, war-baby industries of the nation were destroyed or crippled by the great influx of competitive foreign merchandise, but the new shelf clock business grew by leaps and bounds. Much of the business in the now old-fashioned tall case movements fell away, and their makers entered into competition with Terry, despite the patent he held on his clock. They did this in various ways, the most interesting being the creation of a whole range of evasive designs, involving both movements and cases (a development that must be viewed from our vantage point as evidence of a remarkable versatility and creativity within the industry). Terry's design, however, continued to lead all the others. Following some lawsuits to establish the uniqueness of his patent clock, he evidently licensed a number of rivals.

The 1820's, chiefly, was the period of evasive and innovative designs. With the groundwork thus well laid, the next decade saw a boom in wooden shelf clocks. Several were designed to run for eight days, and nearly all conformed to the new principles patented by Terry. The unique features of this patent were: placing the escapement on the outside of the movement where it was easily accessible for maintenance; placing the gearing for the hands (which never needed attention) out of the way, inside the movement; and carrying the cords for the weights up to the top of the case and over a pulley in such a way that the entire height of the case interior was available for the drop of the weights. Wooden clocks always suffered from certain limitations, however, particularly a fragility of the gear teeth and an affinity for moisture, which could interfere with their accuracy. Thus as wooden clocks were enjoying their greatest vogue, in the 1820's and 30's, a few innovators were devising and marketing clocks with sturdy brass movements. The most advanced of these took advantage of the expanding supply of rolled brass, which could largely be inexpensively fabricated in a press with dies.

When the national economy collapsed in 1837, many of those in the clock business found themselves overextended and failed. So many clocks were thrown on the shrunken market that the clock business itself was virtually destroyed. It was in this period that Chauncey Jerome created his memorable O.G. clock. This was an inexpensive stamped brass striking movement with hour strike housed in a simple but attractive case. The decoration of the case, excluding the tablet in the door, consisted entirely of a molding of ogival form—hence the name O.G.—shaped rather like a mirror or picture frame. This case was ideally suited to very economical manufacture, and the clock remained popular for about as long as pendulum clocks were made, well into the twentieth century. Jerome, who was a master of merchandising, soon developed foreign markets to supplement a flourishing domestic business. Export was possible because of the ruggedness of the metal movement. It not only retained adjustment better than wooden movements, but it was also more durable, even in the hands of the most inept owner. As business revived, brass clocks, in numerous varieties and qualities, left wooden clocks behind. Almost without exception, though, the brass movements perpetuated the basic features of Terry's patents.

Gradually, as clocks became standardized, a few large clockmaking concerns came to dominate the market. Smaller, marginal concerns, no longer able to compete, began to specialize. Out of this situation came many novelty clocks and one totally new production item: the spring-driven movement, in which a balance wheel/hairspring combination, or its equivalent, was substituted for a pendulum. These new clocks were as convenient to operate as a pocket watch. Moreover, they were smaller and more portable than competing clocks because of the absence of weights and pendulum, both of which required that the clock be supported in a steady, vibration-free position. Rapidly growing transportation facilities furnished a considerable part of the market for these spring-driven clocks, and passenger-carrying steam and canal boats gave them their name: they became known as "Marines." Again, as in earlier innovative periods, there was an era of competing designs and producers, followed by a period of general simplification and standardization in the hands of the large manufacturers.

Special tools and primitive machinery had been characteristic of clockmaking throughout the colonial period. Soon after 1800 power-driven machinery was introduced by the makers of wooden clocks. As markets expanded, so did the variety of machines and the facilities for manufacturing them. When the shelf clock was introduced, machine techniques began to be applied to the case too. But as the machinery developed ever-greater sophistication, more and more of the personal touch was eliminated. Good design, which had already degenerated in the search for eye-catching varieties, was now subordinated to the demands of machine production. The culmination of this adaptation of the clock to the machine is seen here in a Jerome-type thirty-hour brass clock in an OG case (No. 44)—by no means the ugliest example. It dates from the period when clockmaking had become quite impersonal, and it is the latest clock in the Yale collection.

By far the greatest part of the Yale collection represents the craftsman-apprentice tradition of clockmaking, the work of 1725 to 1825. Between 1825 and 1865 many diverse types of clocks and new systems of manufacture came into favor during the evolution to full mass production, and transitional types illustrating the changes that took place in this era are also represented (cf. No. 44). By 1865 the skills of the craftsmen had been to some extent adapted to machine manufacture, but the machine could only transfer the same details, over and over—producing, inevitably, an impersonal product.

Even with the hand-crafted clocks we must not delude ourselves in thinking that each of these was entirely the product of the man whose name appears on the dial. We must also recall that clockmakers often employed many apprentices. Toward the end of their indenture these apprentices often became highly skilled, and the direct participation of the master was scarcely needed in producing a clock. Following apprenticeship some became journeymen, but their work still bore their employer's signature. Only when they became self-employed would they sign their work. Thus the only thing we can be reasonably sure of is that the signed clocks represent the standards of the signer. Economic considerations and other factors inevitably intervened between the maker and the highest expression of his ability in a given clock. Cases—usually, or at least frequently, furnished independently—were subject to the same considerations. To develop a rounded concept of any maker's skills we need to study as many examples of his work as possible and to consider many factors, such as competition, sources of supply, and economic conditions prevailing at various times within his market area. Highly individual characteristics can be noted consistently in a series by almost any maker, but snap judgments based on a narrow range of examples may be quite unreliable.

Both hand-crafted and factory-made clocks possess many common features, and it would be redundant to include these in the description of each clock discussed here. For example, the overwhelming majority of tall clocks run for eight days and have brass plates and gears. Lesser parts are of iron and steel. Those parts requiring considerable strength, such as pinions, are usually of steel. Major springs required to supply much force will certainly be of tempered steel. Lesser springs may be of hammered, rolled, or drawn brass, which is also resilient. Screws and similar static elements are almost always made of iron or brass, very rarely of steel. Few cast or malleable iron elements are to be found before the era of the factory-made shelf clock. The exceptions are chiefly weights and the intermediate, or mounting, plate often found between dial and movement in the painted-dial tall clocks that succeeded the earlier brass-dial specimens.

To enter into the minutiae of each clock would exceed the scope of this book and would obscure the really relevant differences—and in the hand-crafted clocks no two were precisely alike, even if by the same maker. Each, whether still entirely in the handcrafted tradition or bridging the gap to totally impersonal machinework, is an entity in a way that no product of our age can be. As such, each clock is a document of an age when the maker, or makers, incorporated some measure of his own personality in the product. □

Note on Woods and Dimensions

All the woods were tested by micro-analysis.

Dimensions for height, width, and depth were taken at the same points (indicated below) for all clocks; they are not necessarily maximum dimensions for a specific clock. Dimensions given are for each clock in its present condition, regardless of damage or restoration.

H. Height.
Case: Measured to the top of center of clock case, including finial if preserved.
Lower case: Measured across upper mold-molding of waist.

MH. Maximum height
Measured to the highest point of clock case if other than at center.

W. Width.
Hood: Measured across the top of cornice.
Lower case: Measured across upper molding of waist.

FW. Frame width.
Hood: Measured just below the cornice molding.
Lower case: Measured just below upper molding of waist.

D. Depth.
Hood: Measured on the top of the left cornice.
Lower case: Measured on the top of the left side of upper molding of waist.

FD. Frame depth.
Hood: Measured on left side, just below the cornice molding
Lower case: Measured on left side, just below upper molding of waist.

tall clocks

tall clocks

CONNECTICUT

1

Fairfield, Connecticut, 1761–1780
"William Burr 2^{d} / of Fairfield Fecit" engraved on dial.

woods
American butternut (*Juglans cinerea*) ; backboard, tulip.

dimensions
CASE: H. 93⅞ in. (238.4 cm) ; hood: W. 20⅛ in. (51.1 cm), FW. 18⅜ in. (46.7 cm), D. 9⅞ in. (25.1 cm), FD. 9 in. (22.9 cm) ; lower case: H. 64 9/16 in. (164.0 cm), W. 18⅛ in. (46.0 cm), FW. 13 15/16 in. (35.4 cm), D. 9 in. (22.9 cm), FD. 6¾ in. (17.1 cm).
DIAL: H. 16¼ in. (41.3 cm), W. 11½ in. (29.2 cm).
MOVEMENT: H. 7½ in. (19.0 cm), W. 5 in. (12.7 cm), D. 2⅞ in. (7.3 cm).

description
Hood with two reel-and-lemon finials, serpentine cornice, frieze with an arch at center front, turned columns at the four corners, rectangular sidelights, and a glazed door with an arched top. Waist with a cove molding at the top and a door with an arched top. Base with a cove molding at the top, a baseboard, cut-out arches on the sides, a double serpentine front skirt, and straight bracket feet.

Wrought brass dial with roman hour numerals, arabic minute numerals, circular punched swagged border surrounding the numerals, engraved flowers in the spandrels and flanking the signature in the arch at the top, calendar, day-of-the-week and month-of-the year apertures below unusual pierced hands.

Eight-day movement with brass plates and wheels, cut pinions, winding drums unusually high in the plates, seconds pendulum with anchor-recoil escapement, two double-hung crank key wound weights, holes at the bottom of front plate for dial feet never fitted to dial, and a count wheel striking system.

condition
Finials and domed pediment replaced; feet on left side restored; feet on right side repaired; new corner blocks; sidelights cracked; case refinished.

Dial dented and bent; second hand missing; calendar disc missing; day-of-the-week and month-of-the-year dials missing; bell missing; movement coarsely made and worn.

provenance
Found in Trumbull, Conn.; Henry H. Taylor, Bridgeport, Conn.; Francis P. Garvan, New York, N.Y.

comments
William Burr 2d of Fairfield, whose name is engraved on the dial of this clock, was born on July 23, 1740, and may have trained with his uncle, Nathaniel (1707–1784), an early Fairfield, Connecticut, watchmaker and jeweler. How long he worked in Fairfield is not known, but he probably began his independent career as a clockmaker sometime after he was twenty-one in 1761. Unfortunately the younger Burr was not a very proficient craftsman, if we are to judge from the present example. On the dial the feathered flourishes on the "W" and "B" have a certain charm, but the engraving is wispy and childlike in character. The pierced steel hands are finished with individual detail, but mistakes on the numerals 40, 50, and XI were not corrected skillfully. The domed top of the case is new; the cornice molding may have terminated originally in a swan neck pediment. The case is made of butternut, a wood not often used on Connecticut furniture.

The Mabel Brady Garvan Collection
1930.2173

of
Fairfield
55
60

William Burr
of Fairfield Fecit

2

Norwich area, Connecticut, about 1775
"R = Ingraham / Preston" engraved on dial.

woods
Soft maple; finials, American black walnut; frame surrounding clock face, tulip; backboard and secondary wood in hood, white pine; blocks in base, pine of the *Taeda* group and chestnut.

dimensions
CASE: H. 89⅛ in. (226.4 cm); lower case: H. 62⅞ in. (159.7 cm), W. 17¹¹⁄₁₆ in. (44.9 cm), FW. 12 in. (30.5 cm), D. 9¾ in. (24.8 cm), FD. 7 in. (17.8 cm).
DIAL: H. 16 in. (41.1 cm), W. 11¾ in. (29.5 cm).
MOVEMENT: H. 6½ in. (16.5 cm), W. 4⅞ in. (12.4 cm), D. 2⅝ in. (6.7 cm).

description
Hood with three turned pagoda-like finials—the outer two on fluted plinths—swan neck pediment with carved rosettes, spiral turned columns at the front corners, and a glazed door with an arched top. Waist with a cove molding at the top, and a door with an arched top. Three-part base with a cove molding at the top, and ogee and cove molding at the center, and ogee and cove molding above the baseboard.

Wrought brass dial with roman hour numerals, arabic minute numerals, engraved arabesques in the spandrels, center, and around the signature in the arch at the top; seconds dial above pierced hands and calendar aperture below.

Eight-day movement with brass plates and wheels, cut pinions, seconds pendulum with anchor-recoil escapement, grooved winding drums, two double-hung weights, and a rack and snail repeating striking system.

condition
Central finial replaced; side pieces of board surrounding clock face replaced; case refinished. Second hand missing; dial very wavy; dial feet re-riveted; bell and hanger missing; time train rebushed with modern friction bushings.

provenance
Francis P. Garvan, New York, N.Y.

exhibitions
Hartford, Conn., Wadsworth Atheneum, Nov. 3–Dec. 17, 1967, *Connecticut Furniture: Seventeenth and Eighteenth Centuries,* p. 147, no. 263 (illus. p. 146).

bibliography
Wallace Nutting, *Furniture Treasury,* no. 3324; Penrose R. Hoopes, "Some Minor Connecticut Clockmakers," *Antiques,* 27 (Sept. 1935), 105, fig. 1; Ada R. Chase, "Two Eighteenth-Century Clockmakers," *Antiques,* 38 (Sept. 1940), p. 117, fig. 4; Meyric R. Rogers, "The Mabel Brady Garvan Collection of Furniture," *Yale Alumni Magazine,* 25 (Jan. 1962), illus. p. 15).

comments
Five tall clocks with dials inscribed by Reuben Ingraham are known. Ingraham, born in 1743 or 1744 in Saybrook, Connecticut, grew up in Preston, where he probably served an apprenticeship with the local clockmaker, John Avery. This example is one of two Ingraham clocks inscribed "Preston." "Plainfield" appears on two others. The Preston clocks were undoubtedly made before Ingraham and John Avery (a relative of the Preston clockmaker), both "Goldsmiths," purchased land and buildings in Plainfield on October 8, 1784 (Ada R. Chase, *Antiques,* Sept. 1940, p. 116). Ingraham continued to live in Plainfield until his death on June 14, 1811. The carved rosettes on the swan neck pediment, pagoda-shaped finials, rope turned columns, and the turned, acorn-shaped escutcheon on the door reveal the hand of an ingenious Connecticut cabinetmaker. The case exemplifies the individualism and inventiveness of much of the furniture made in that rural society. The case of a Thomas Harland clock, made by Abishai Woodward, a Preston joiner, has a similar hooded pediment and carved rosettes (Ada R. Chase and Houghton Bulkeley, "Thomas Harland's Clock—Whose Case?" *Antiques,* June 1965, pp. 700–701). A comparison of the engraving on this dial with other Connecticut examples reveals that this dial is finished quite expertly.

The Mabel Brady Garvan Collection
1930.2285

R Ingraham
PRESTON

3

Fairfield, Connecticut, 1787–1791
"Whiting & Marquand / Fairfield" engraved on dial.

wood
Tulip.

dimensions
CASE: H. 88⅝ in. (225.1 cm); hood: W. 19⁷⁄₁₆ in. (49.9 cm), FW. 17⅝ in. (44.8 cm), D. 10¾ in. (27.4 cm), FD. 9⅞ in. (25.1 cm); lower case: H. 62⁷⁄₁₆ in. (158.6 cm), W. 18¼ in. (46.4 cm), FW. 12¼ in. (31.1 cm), D. 11¼ in. (28.6 cm), FD. 8⅛ in. (20.6 cm).
DIAL: H. 16½ in. (41.9 cm), W. 12 in. (30.5 cm).
MOVEMENT: H. 7 in. (17.8 cm), W. 5 in. (12.7 cm), D. 2⅞ in. (7.3 cm).

description
Hood with a flat, ogee-molded cornice, a frieze with an arch at the center front, turned balusters at the four corners, oval sidelights, and a glazed door with an arched top. Waist with a cove molding at the top, and a door with an arched top. Base with a cove and ogee molding at the top, and a baseboard with an ogee arch at the center of the front.

Wrought brass dial with roman hour numerals, arabic minute numerals, spandrels engraved with candles, urns, and flowers; oval frame for signature in arch at the top, an inset seconds dial above the pierced gilded hands and a four-inch calendar disc and aperture below.

Eight-day movement with brass plates and wheels, cut pinions, seconds pendulum with anchor-recoil escapement, double-hung crank key wound weights, and a rack and snail striking system.

condition
Hinges and keeper replaced on case door; crack on front of base repaired; later graining and painted decoration; finials missing; lower hinge of hood door replaced.

Seconds and calendar dials appear to have been nickel plated; minute hand repaired; second hand replaced; seconds dial engraved on both sides; numbers on back are in reverse sequence.

Movement worn, has been through the hands of a rough workman; iron and steel rusted and pitted; movement does not fit perfectly in case, left end of seat board requiring ¼-inch riser.

provenance
According to tradition Thaddeus Burr (1735–1801) Fairfield, Conn.; descended to Katherine Birks Prevost [Fairfield, Conn.?]; Henry H. Taylor, Bridgeport, Conn.; Francis P. Garvan, New York, N.Y. (1929).

comments
This clock was made between 1787 and 1791, when Isaac Marquand of Fairfield, Connecticut, and a B. Whiting, perhaps the Norwich silversmith of that name, were in partnership as clockmakers (Flynt and Fales, *Heritage Foundation Coll.*, p. 272). At least two clocks inscribed with their names are known (Penrose R. Hoopes, "Some Minor Connecticut Clockmakers," *Antiques*, 27 [September 1935], p. 104). The dial may have been engraved by Whiting, for its curious design of candles or columnar forms and puffy circles seems to be derived from the more expertly finished dials of two other Norwich craftsmen, Thomas Harland (Hoopes, fig. 18) and Nathaniel Shipman (Hoopes, fig. 22), either of whom may have trained Whiting. Marquand, who was apprenticed to his uncle Jacob Jennings, a Norwalk, Connecticut, silversmith, established his own business in Fairfield in 1787. He worked there until 1791, when he moved to Edenton, N.C., where he advertised as a goldsmith, silversmith, clockmaker and watchmaker. In 1796 he returned to Fairfield but subsequently settled in New York. The case was probably made by a Fairfield joiner. Its arched frieze, flat pediment, and heavy baseboard with double serpentine curves seem uncommonly massive for a piece of furniture made so late in the eighteenth century. This clock is said to have been owned by Thaddeus Burr. The inventory of his estate, taken in 1801, reveals that he owned "1 clock & case $40"; this was his most expensive piece of personal property (Fairfield Probate District, no. 1425, at the Connecticut State Library).

The Mabel Brady Garvan Collection
1930.2287

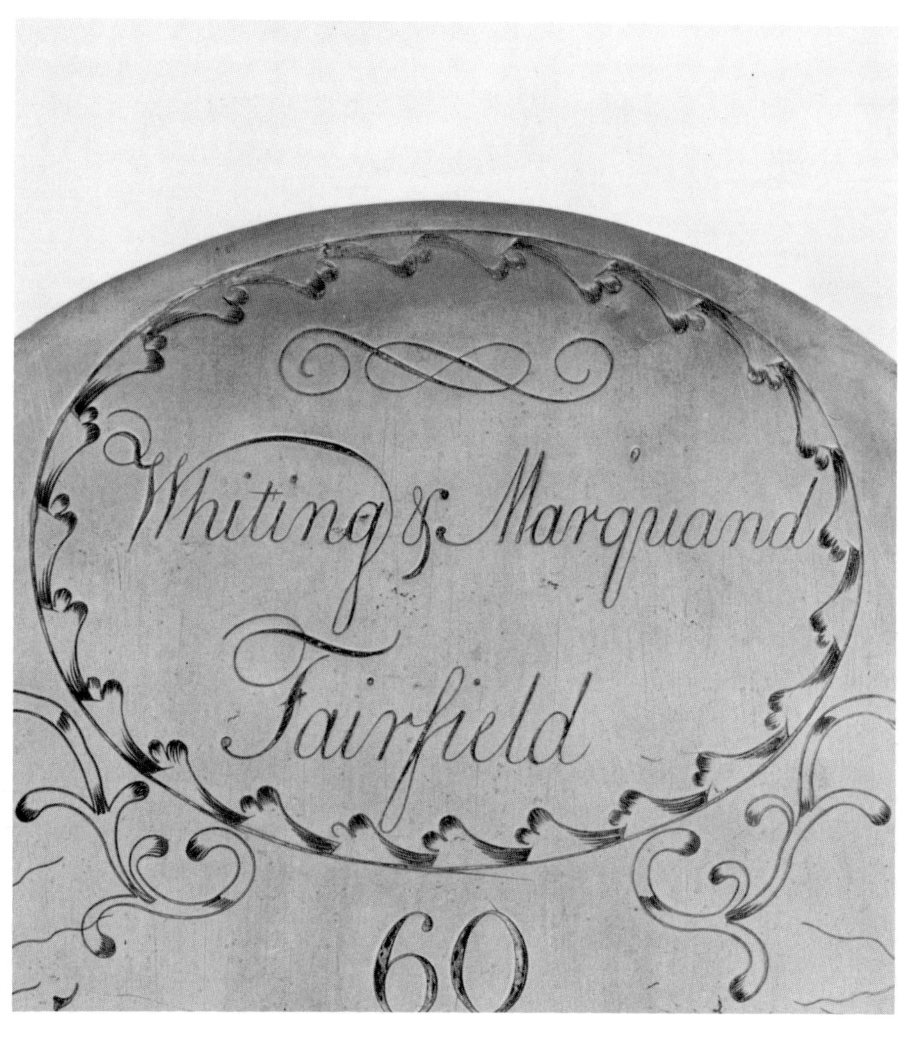
Whiting & Marquand
Fairfield
60

Whiting & Marquand
Fairfield

tall clocks

CONNECTICUT

Probably Windsor, Connecticut, about 1790
"Thomas Lyman / Windsor" engraved on dial.

woods
American butternut; top and base of hood, white pine.

dimensions
CASE: H. 86 15/16 in. (220.8 cm); hood: W. 17 7/8 in. (45.5 cm), D. 10 1/8 in. (25.7 cm); lower case: H. 59 3/4 in. (151.8 cm), W. 17 7/8 in. (45.4 cm), FW. 12 11/16 in. (32.2 cm), D. 10 3/8 in. (26.4 cm), FD. 7 7/8 in. (20.0 cm).
DIAL: H. 16 3/8 in. (41.6 cm), W. 12 in. (30.5 cm).
MOVEMENT: H. 6 1/4 in. (15.9 cm), W. 5 in. (12.7 cm), D. 2 5/8 in. (6.7 cm).

description
Hood with three spired urn finials, a swan neck pediment, frieze with an arch at center front, molded pilasters at the front corners, and a glazed door with an arched top. Waist with a double cove molding at the top and a door with canted upper corners. Base with cove and ogee moldings at the top, serpentine skirts on the front and sides, and French feet.

Silvered wrought brass dial with roman hour numerals, arabic minute numerals, engraved arabesques in the spandrels, at the center, and around signature in the arched top; seconds dial above the pierced hands and calendar aperture below.

Eight-day movement with brass plates and wheels, cut pinions, seconds pendulum with anchor-recoil escapement, grooved drums, two double-hung weights, and rack and snail striking system.

condition
Center of the bottom board missing; plinth for right finial restored; tops of two finials missing; new hinges on the glazed door; one dial foot replaced; considerable wear; minute hand repaired; weight pulleys old, but mismated.

provenance
Francis P. Garvan, New York, N.Y.

comments
This clock engraved with the name "Thomas Lyman/Windsor" is a rare example of this clockmaker's work, for Lyman, born in Coventry, Connecticut, in 1770, and trained by the East Windsor clockmaker Daniel Burnap, left Connecticut for Ohio almost immediately after finishing his apprenticeship. The engraving on the dial is obviously derived from the designs used by his master (Hoopes, *Conn. Clockmakers*, fig. 28). Both this and the Burnap dial have trees on mounds of earth at the base and an oval with ribbons surrounding the signature, although the engraving on Burnap's is more expert. The brass plates in the movement, which have ogee arches at the bottom and arched corners at the top, are extra heavy. This is a fine example of an American-made clock that has very few imported parts. The construction of the pine case is extremely simple, with little attention paid to fine details.

The Mabel Brady Garvan Collection
1931.1246

50
10
40
20
30
25
27
23
29

Thomas Lyman
Windsor

tall clocks
CONNECTICUT

5

East Windsor area, Connecticut, 1792–1793
"Terry E. Windsor" engraved on dial.

woods
Cherry; backboard and top of hood, white pine.

dimensions
CASE: H. 95½ in. (242.6 cm); hood: W. 19 in. (48.3 cm), FW. 17⅝ in. (44.8 cm), D. 11¼ in. (28.6 cm), FD. 10⅝ in. (27.0 cm); lower case: H. 60½ in. (153.7 cm), W. 17⅞ in. (45.4 cm), FW. 12 in. (30.5 cm), D. 10⅞ in. (27.6 cm), FD. 7¹³⁄₁₆ in. (19.8 cm).
DIAL: H. 17⅛ in. (43.5 cm), W. 12 in. (30.5 cm).
MOVEMENT: H. 10½ in. (26.7 cm), W. 8⅜ in. (21.3 cm), D. 4¼ in. (10.8 cm).

description
Hood with three lemon-shaped spired finials—the outer two on fluted plinths—pagoda-shaped pediment with applied fretwork, a frieze with an arch at center front, freestanding columns at the corners, arched sidelights, and a glazed door with an arched top. Waist with a cove molding at the top, fluted quarter columns at the front corners, and a door with a double serpentine top. Base with a cove molding at the top, square of applied molding at the front, and a three-part molded baseboard.

Wrought brass dial with roman hour numerals, arabic minute numerals, engraved arabesques in the spandrels, at the center, and around the arched top; a seconds dial above the pierced hands and calendar aperture below; engraved global maps flank moon dial painted with a blue ground and stars.

A twenty-four-hour movement with oak plates, lenticular cherry train wheels, maple pillars, hickory main arbors, other arbors and pinions birch, cherry center post; center post passing entirely through the movement, driven from main wheel, contra-wound winding cords, count wheel with locking notches between gear teeth and backplate controls striking system, brass escape wheel, anchor-recoil escapement for seconds pendulum.

condition
Fretwork repaired; right side of hood cracked; front of base with repaired crack; lower case door restored in lower left corner; new hinges on lower case door; case refinished in 1964. Two teeth in the cherry count wheel replaced with birch with the grain at right angles; ratchets replaced on both winding drums; ratchet click and pin on time side replaced; second hand possibly replaced.

provenance
Frank MacCarthy, Longmeadow, Mass.; Francis P. Garvan, New York, N.Y. (1929).

exhibitions
Conn. Furn., p. 147, no. 264 (illus. p. 146).

bibliography
"American Furniture . . .", *Handbook of the Gallery of Fine Arts* (Associates in Fine Arts at Yale University), 5, (1931), 59 (illus.); Charles Nagel, *American Furniture, 1650–1850,* New York: Chanticleer Press, 1949, p. 54, pl. 22b; Hoopes, *Conn. Clockmakers,* nos. 27 and 52.

comments
The East Windsor clockmaker Eli Terry (1772–1852) was trained by Daniel Burnap and ran his own clockmaking business in East Windsor from 1792 until September, 1793, when he moved to Plymouth, Connecticut. There he established his factory for making shelf clocks with wooden works. Terry's first tall clocks were fitted with silvered brass dials engraved for him by Burnap (Hoopes, *Conn. Clockmakers*, p. 113). Whereas Burnap specialized in brass-wheeled clocks, Terry seems to have made his movements of wood as well as brass from the first. It has been suggested that Terry may have learned to make wooden clocks with Timothy Cheney of East Hartford (Hoopes, *Conn. Clockmakers,* p. 112). The relatively plain cherry case of this clock is crowned with a pagoda-shaped pediment and pierced fretwork influenced by the Chinese taste. Like his master, Terry probably employed journeyman cabinetmakers to make cases for him. In 1795 Burnap advertised for such a craftsman to make fifteen or twenty cases (Hoopes, *Conn. Clockmakers,* p. 56).

The Mabel Brady Garvan Collection
1930.2199

Perry
E. Windsor

tall clocks

DELAWARE

Probably Wilmington, Delaware, about 1800

"Jonas Alrichs / WILMINGTON." painted on dial.

woods

Mahogany; top of hood, tulip; glueblock in hood, white pine.

dimensions

CASE: H. 101⅝ in. (258.1 cm); hood: W. 21¾ in. (55.3 cm), FW. 19⅛ in. (48.6 cm), D. 11 in. (27.9 cm), FD. 9⅝ in. (24.5 cm); lower case: H. 69⅛ in. (175.6 cm), W. 19 in. (48.3 cm), FW. 13 11/16 in. (34.8 cm), D. 10 1/16 in. (25.6 cm), FD. 7¼ in. (18.4 cm).
DIAL: H. 18½ in. (40.7 cm), W. 13 in. (33.0 cm).
MOVEMENT: H. 6⅞ in. (17.5 cm), W. 4⅞ in. (12.4 cm), D. 2⅝ in. (6.6 cm).

inscription

IE: branded three times on backboard; "ASHWIN & CO." cast on secondary plate between dial and movement.

description

Hood with three cup-and-spired finials—the outer two on fluted plinths—a swan neck pediment with carved rosettes, a frieze with a drapery swag and arch at center front, free-standing fluted columns at the four corners, arched sidelights, and a glazed door with an arched top. Waist with a cove molding at the top, a band of veneer at the top and bottom, fluted quarter columns at the front corners, and a door with an arched top. Base with a cove molding at the top, fluted quarter columns at the front corners, and ogee bracket feet.

Painted iron dial with roman hour numerals, arabic minute numerals, gilded paterae and arabesques in the spandrels, seconds dial above the pierced hands and calendar aperture below, and transfer-printed global maps flanking moon dial.

Eight-day movement with brass plates and wheels, cut pinions, anchor-recoil escapement, grooved drums, two double-hung weights, rack and snail repeating striking system, and large disc with pins to actuate calendar and moon dials.

condition

Hinges replaced on waist door; top of center finial restored; feet and corner blocks replaced; case refinished in 1964; paint abraded on dial; surface of dial very dirty; winding hole grommet missing from the time side; moon dial repainted; some wear; second hand replaced.

provenance

Francis P. Garvan, New York, N.Y.

comments

Jonas Alrichs was born in 1759 and worked in Wilmington, Delaware, from 1772 until his retirement, announced in 1797. For part of that time (1793–1797) he was in partnership with a nephew, Jacob, who succeeded him in the business (Gibbs, p. 713). This clock was probably made in the years just prior to the partnership. The case has hints of the neoclassical style in the small carved drapery swag beneath the central finial and in the bands of dark veneer applied to the top and bottom of the waist, although its ogee-bracket feet and fluted quarter columns are in the older taste. The inside of the backboard is branded "IE" three times. These initials may be those of John or James Erwin, cabinetmakers, in Wilmington. John Erwin, the father, operated a shop from 1751 until his death in 1797, and his son James helped him and took over the business when his father died (Charles G. Dorman, "Delaware Cabinetmakers and Allied Artisans, 1655–1855," *Delaware History*, Wilmington, 1960, pp. 136–137). The skeleton mounting plate bears the name "Ashwin & Co." The pinwheel drive of the calendar and moon discs is sufficiently unique to be original to the clockmaker.

The Mabel Brady Garvan Collection
1930.2085

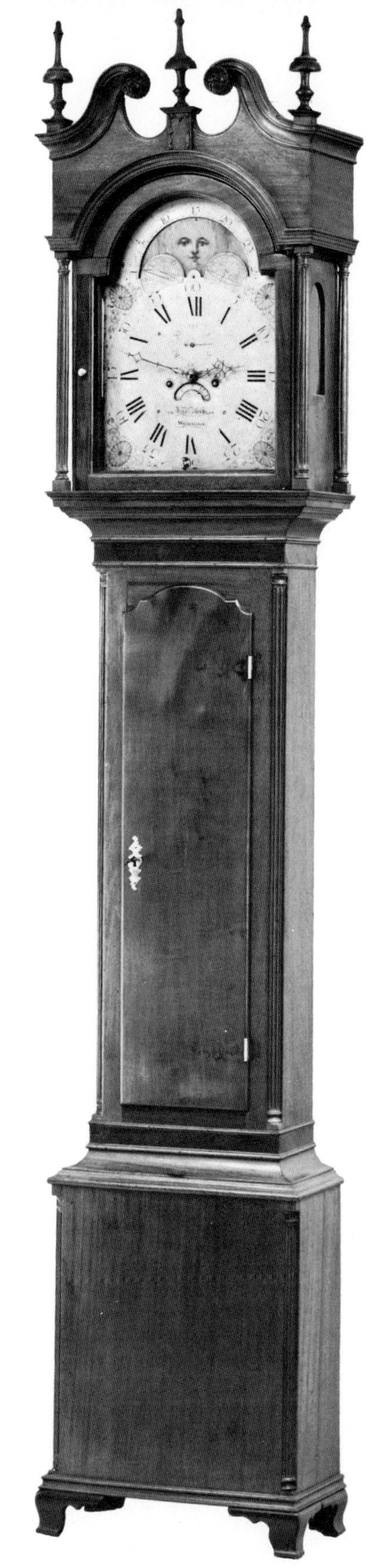

Jonas Alrichs
WILMINGTON

tall clocks

DISTRICT OF COLUMBIA

7

Possibly Georgetown, District of Columbia, 1765–1785

"CHRISTOPHER•WEAVER:GEORGE:TOWN" engraved on dial.

woods

Mahogany; top of hood, tulip; back of hood, pine of the *Taeda* group.

dimensions

CASE: H. 96½ in. (245.1 cm); hood: W. 20½ in. (52.1 cm), FW. 18¼ in. (46.4 cm), D. 10⅜ in. (26.4 cm), FD. 9⅝ in. (24.5 cm); lower case: H. 71⅜ in. (181.3 cm), W. 19³⁄₁₆ in. (48.7 cm), FW. 13¹³⁄₁₆ in. (35.1 cm), D. 9¾ in. (24.8 cm), FD. 7⅛ in. (18.1 cm).
DIAL: H. 16⅞ in. (42.9 cm), W. 12⅛ in. (31.3 cm).
MOVEMENT: H. 6½ in. (16.5 cm), W. 4¹⁵⁄₁₆ in. (12.6 cm), D. 2¾ in. (7.0 cm).

description

Hood with a flat top, band of fretwork on the frieze, fluted columns at the four corners, arched sidelights with latticework, and a glazed door with an arched top. Waist with a cove molding at the top, fluted quarter columns and a door with serpentine curved top. Base with cove and ovolo moldings at the top, fluted quarter columns at the front corners, an applied panel with serpentine curved edges, and ogee bracket feet.

Wrought brass dial with roman hour numerals, arabic minute and second numerals on an applied chapter ring, red painted pewter ornaments in the spandrels, signature plate in the arch above the moon dial, global map and rising sun in front of moon dial, floral engraving at center of main dial, and day-of-the-month aperture below pierced hour and minute hands.

Eight-day key wound movement with brass wheels and pinions, seconds pendulum with anchor-recoil escapement, grooved drums, two double-hung weights, and a rack and snail repeating striking system.

condition

Left cornice molding and corner restored; feet and corner blocks replaced; top molding of lower case replaced; small patch in lower case door at right base; shrinkage crack repaired in front panel of base; case refinished in 1964; dial bent; some filling missing from engraving; second hand missing; crude spandrels probably replaced.

provenance

Francis P. Garvan, New York, N.Y.

comments

The clockmaker, Christopher Weaver, is not mentioned in any of the standard reference books on American clocks, and the location of the Georgetown in which he worked is impossible to identify positively, although it may have been in the District of Columbia. The cabinetwork of the case exhibits the influence of the Philadelphia style with its fluted quarter columns, fretwork at the top of the hood, and applied serpentine curved plaque at the base of the case. The movement itself is quite individual. The extra reinforcing disc behind the moon dial has a few circular grooves divided by punchmarks, and it may once have been intended as an index plate in a wheel-cutting engine. The ears, or projections, on the front plate to which the upper dial feet are attached are an unusual feature. These ears are similar to those often encountered on clocks of the Philadelphia maker Edward Duffield, and they appear in at least one clock by Frederick Dominick of Philadelphia.

The Mabel Brady Garvan Collection
1930.2022

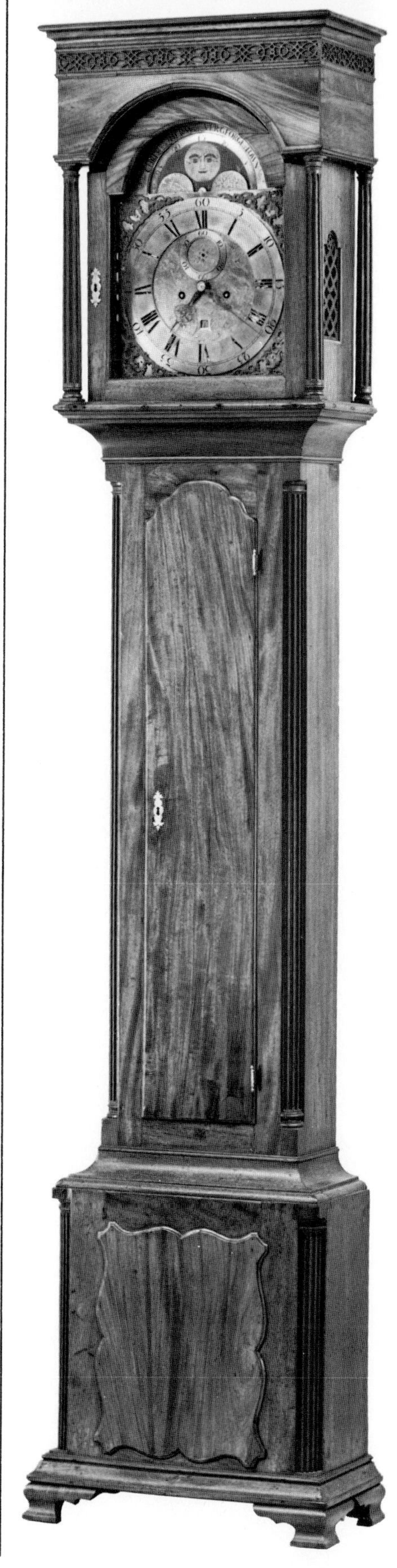

CHRISTOPHER·WEAVER·GEORGE·TOWN

tall clocks

MAINE

Augusta, Maine, about 1810

"Frederick Wingate / Augusta / N°217" painted on dial.

woods

Maple and mahogany veneer; white pine; basswood; soft maple.

dimensions

CASE: H. 95 in. (241.3 cm); hood: W. 19⅝ in. (49.9 cm), FW. 15½ in. (39.4 cm), D. 9½ in. (24.2 cm); lower case: H. 63 13/16 in. (162.1 cm), W. 19 7/16 in. (49.4 cm), FW. 13⅞ in. (35.2 cm), D. 10⅛ in. (25.7 cm), FD. 7¼ in. (18.4 cm).
DIAL: H. 16¼ in. (41.8 cm), W. 12 in. (30.5 cm).
MOVEMENT: H. 6⅝ in. (16.8 cm), W. 4⅞ in. (12.4 cm), D. 2¾ in. (7.0 cm).

description

Hood with three brass spired ball finials on fluted plinths, fretwork, cornice with an arch at the front, rectangular sidelights, bulbous turned columns at the front corners, and a glazed door with an arch at the top. Waist with a cove molding at the top, fluted quarter columns, and a door with bird's-eye maple and mahogany veneer. Base with cove molding at the top, a recessed panel at the front, triple arched molding on the front and sides, serpentine skirts, and French feet.

Painted iron dial with roman hour numerals, arabic minute numerals, painted fruit and gilt arabesques in the spandrels, painted and gilt urn and swags in the arch at the top, seconds dial above the center of the main dial, an arched calendar aperture below, and pierced hour and minute hands.

Eight-day movement with brass plates with rounded arches at the bottom, brass wheels, cut pinions, a second pendulum with anchor-recoil escapement, grooved drums, double-hung weights, and a rack and snail striking system.

condition

Fretwork repaired; upper right corner of hood door patched; new corner blocks on front feet; case refinished. Paint abraded particularly on the upper right corner of the dial, which has been bent; second hand replaced; pivot holes worn; pallets loose on arbor.

provenance

Francis P. Garvan, New York, N.Y.

comments

Frederick Wingate was born in Haverhill, Massachusetts, but settled in Augusta, Maine, during the early years of the nineteenth century. This case, with its fretwork on the pediment, and door with bird's-eye maple and mahogany crossbanding, reflects the high-style designs of Massachusetts furniture-making centers as they were interpreted by Maine's more provincial craftsmen. The dial may possibly be from the workshop of Spencer Nolen and Samuel Curtis, who worked in Roxbury, Massachusetts, ca. 1805–1810. A Pennsylvania clock bears a label of theirs with similar urn and swag designs and heavy gold beading.

The Mabel Brady Garvan Collection
1930.2328

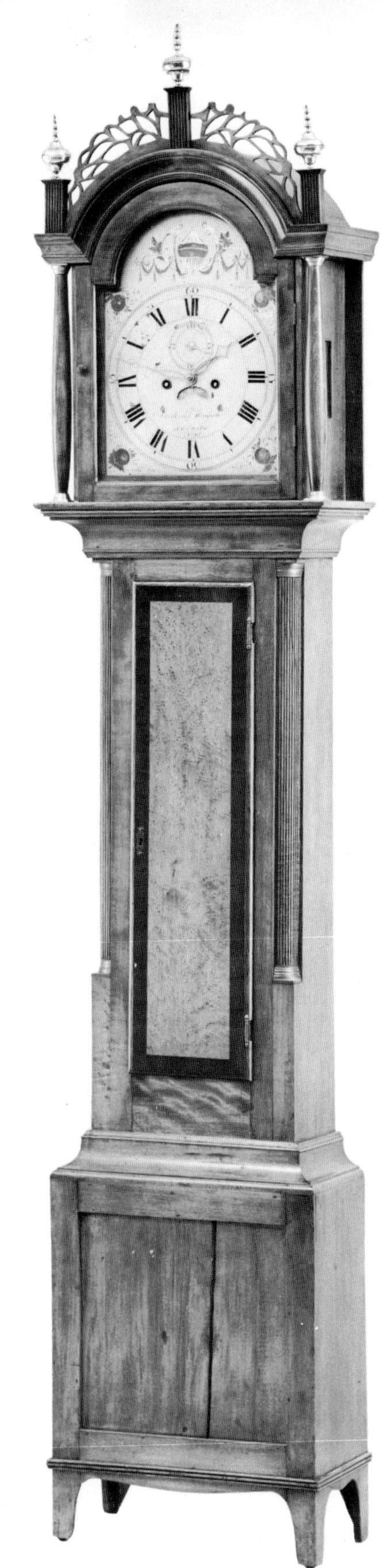

Frederick Wingate
Augusta
No. 217

tall clocks
MASSACHUSETTS

Grafton, Massachusetts, 1773–1775
"Benjamin Willard, / Grafton." painted on dial.

woods
American cherry; backboard, white pine.

dimensions
CASE: H. 91⅞ in. (233.4 cm); hood: W. 21 in. (53.4 cm), D. 12½ in. (31.8 cm); lower case: H. 60⅞ in. (154.6 cm), W. 19¼ in. (48.9 cm), FW. 14⅜ in. (36.5 cm), D. 11⅜ in. (28.9 cm), FD. 8⅞ in. (22.5 cm). *DIAL:* H. 18½ in. (47.0 cm), W. 13 in. (33.0 cm).
MOVEMENT: H. 7½ in. (19.0 cm), W. 7 in. (17.8 cm), D. 2¾ in. (9.5 cm).

inscription
Painted on innermost circle of dial, clockwise from twelve: "Orpheus. Marquis of Granby. Duke of Argyle. Paddy Whack. New Jersey. Mrs. Casey. Pleasures of Solitude." "Osborne's / MANUFACTORY / BIRMINGHAM" cast in false plate of iron behind dial.

description
Hood with three brass spired ball finials on fluted plinths, applied fretwork, cornice with an arch at center front, freestanding fluted columns at the front corners, applied molding at the rear corners, arched sidelights, and a glazed door with an arched top. Waist with a cove molding on the top, fluted quarter columns at the front corners, and a door with a serpentine curved top. Base with a cove molding at the top and ogee bracket feet.

Painted iron dial with roman hour numerals, arabic minute numerals, floral sprays in the spandrels, transfer-printed global maps flanking the moon dial, seconds dial above the pierced hands and calendar dial below, and names of songs below the hour numerals.

Eight-day movement with extra-heavy brass plates, additional partial plate behind the main plates carried by extra pillars to support music barrel, a string of ten bells and a fan governor with three blades; brass wheels, cut pinions, seconds pendulum with anchor-recoil escapement, grooved winding drums, three double-hung weights, and a rack and snail striking system. Music barrel (2½ in. diameter by 4¾ in. long) shifts endwise to each successive selection automatically every hour or manually by means of a special hand on dial and a pull cord. Wide gear on pin barrel and width of narrow gear it engages indicates extent of this end motion.

condition
Corner block and back of right rear foot restored; new glueblocks in base; front of right front foot restored; fretwork on right side of hood repaired; case refinished. Dial paint chipped over one dial foot; paint yellowed from a coat of shellac or varnish; second hand missing; some wear evident, particularly in pivot holes of striking train; lever to start music manually missing.

provenance
R. W. Somerville, New York, N.Y.; Francis P. Garvan, New York, N.Y. (1929).

comments
Benjamin Willard, the oldest member of the famous family of Massachusetts clockmakers, may have learned his trade from the East Hartford clockmaker Benjamin Cheney before purchasing land in Grafton, Massachusetts, in 1764. Seven years later Willard opened a branch of his business in Roxbury. Advertisements in the *Boston Gazette* from 1773 to 1775 indicate that in those years Willard was making musical clocks "that go by spring, also Musical Clocks that go by weights and play a different Tune each Day in the Week, on Sunday's a Psalm Tune,"—a description that seems to apply perfectly to this clock (Willard, Plate 28, opposite p. 78). The case is of cherry, a wood not often found on Massachusetts furniture. It lends a soft, warm color to this case with fluted quarter columns, arched cornice, and delicate fretwork so characteristic of the cases of the Roxbury clocks of Benjamin's younger brothers, Simon and Aaron.

The Mabel Brady Garvan Collection
1930.2284

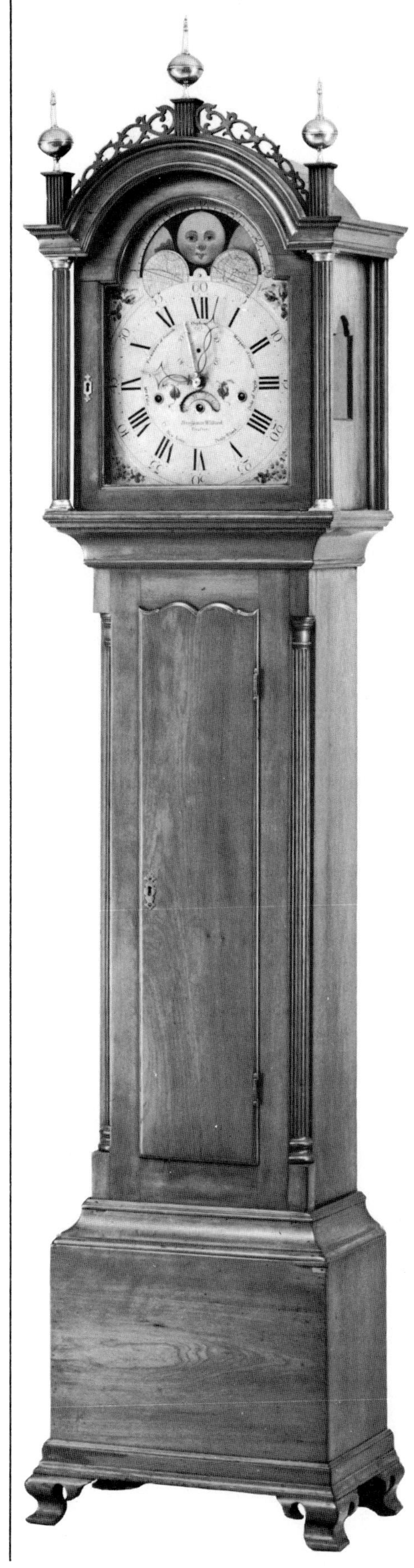

Orpheus
Pleasures of Solitude
Marquis of Granby
Mrs Caſey
Duke of Argyle
Benjamin Willard,
Grafton.
New Jerſey
Paddy Whack

tall clocks

MASSACHUSETTS

Massachusetts, 1772–1782

"Jo^{n} Mulliken / Newbury Port" engraved on dial.

woods

American butternut; top back of hood, white pine.

dimensions

CASE: H. $79\frac{5}{8}$ in. (202.2 cm); hood: W. $21\frac{3}{8}$ in. (54.3 cm), FW. $15\frac{7}{8}$ in. (40.4 cm), D. $10\frac{3}{16}$ in. (25.9 cm); lower case: H. $56\frac{1}{16}$ in. (142.4 cm), W. $19\frac{3}{4}$ in. (50.2 cm), FW. 14 in. (35.6 cm), D. $10\frac{3}{8}$ in. (26.4 cm), FD. $7\frac{7}{16}$ in. (18.9 cm).
DIAL: H. $16\frac{3}{8}$ in. (41.6 cm), W. $11\frac{7}{8}$ in. (30.2 cm).
MOVEMENT: H. $6\frac{1}{2}$ in. (16.5 cm), W. $4\frac{11}{16}$ in. (11.9 cm), D. $2\frac{5}{8}$ in. (6.7 cm).

description

Hood with a cornice with an arch at center front, two freestanding columns at the front corners, quarter columns at the rear corners, arched sidelights, and a glazed door with an arched top. Waist with a cove molding at the top and a door with an arched top. Base with a cove molding at the top and a baseboard with a double arch on each side and a central scallop and serpentine curves in front.

Wrought brass dial with roman hour numerals and arabic minute numerals engraved on a brass chapter ring, cast brass rococo ornaments in the spandrels and flanking the signature plate in the arch at the top, stippled center, inset seconds dial above the pierced hour hand and calendar aperture below.

Eight-day movement with brass plates and wheels, cut pinions, seconds pendulum with anchor-recoil escapement, two double-hung weights, grooved winding drums, crank key for winding, and a rack and snail striking system.

condition

New corner blocks; hood door reglazed; right front foot restored; finials missing; case refinished in 1963; minute hand missing; movement worn, pivot holes mutilated by punch marks; center wheel needs repair.

provenance

Henry H. Taylor, Bridgeport, Conn.; Francis P. Garvan, New York, N.Y.

comments

This tall clock was made between 1772 and 1782, when Jonathan Mulliken (1746–1782) operated a shop in Newburyport, Massachusetts. The walnut wood and cove molded arched top make the case seem somehow stylistically earlier than Mulliken's working dates would suggest. In particular, the broad, stocky proportions and the double arches on the side skirts, shaped like the sides of early eighteenth-century highchests, seem *retardataire* and lack the lightness and delicacy of the rococo style.

The Mabel Brady Garvan Collection
1930.2331

Jon Mulliken
Newbury Port

Jon Mulliken
Newbury Port

Ipswich, Massachusetts, 1793

"Aaron Smith, 1793" engraved on disc in overarch, now missing.

wood

White pine.

dimensions

CASE: H. 82 in. (208.3 cm); hood: W. 20½ in. (52.1 cm), FW. 15 15/16 in. (40.9 cm), D. 12¼ in. (31.2 cm), D. 9¾ in. (24.8 cm); lower case: H. 58¼ in. (147.9 cm), W. 17¼ in. (43.8 cm), FW. 12¼ in. (31.1 cm), D. 11 in. (27.9 cm), FD. 8 in. (20.3 cm). *DIAL:* H. 15 in. (38.1 cm), W. 11 in. (27.9 cm). *MOVEMENT:* H. 6¼ in. (15.9 cm), W. 5¾ in. (14.6 cm), D. 5 in. (12.7 cm).

description

Hood with a flat cove-molded pediment, a frieze with an arch at center front, columnar turnings at each of the four corners, and a glazed door with an arched top. Waist with a cove molding at the top and a door with an arched top. Base with a cove and ovolo molding at the top and a baseboard around the bottom.

Wrought brass dial with roman hour numerals, arabic minute numerals, cast cherubs' heads and arabesques in the spandrels and cast floral arabesques in the overarch.

A thirty-hour movement attached to dial with an angle bracket with iron posts, trains arranged front to back, brass wheels and bearing pieces for arbors, cut pinions, contra-winding cords, smooth drums, count-wheel striking system and anchor-recoil escapement for seconds pendulum.

condition

Traces of old red paint on case heavily cleaned and refinished; baseboard on right side and latch of lower case door missing; dial lacks one spandrel and the signature cartouche from the overarch reported lost in 1965; hands missing; pallet arbor bent to bring pallets closer to escape wheel; binding nut from a #6 dry cell holds the bell in place; generally good running condition.

provenance

Francis P. Garvan, New York, N.Y.

comments

Palmer reports that Aaron Smith was active in Ipswich, Massachusetts, from 1775 to 1785, and that he made bayonets for the Revolutionary army (*Am. Clocks,* p. 278). The overarch on the dial of this clock at one time had a disc engraved with the name of the maker and the date 1793. The thirty-hour contra-winding device often found on earlier metal clocks (see No. 33) and later wooden movement clocks of New England is unusual in a movement of this date.

The Mabel Brady Garvan Collection
1930.2335

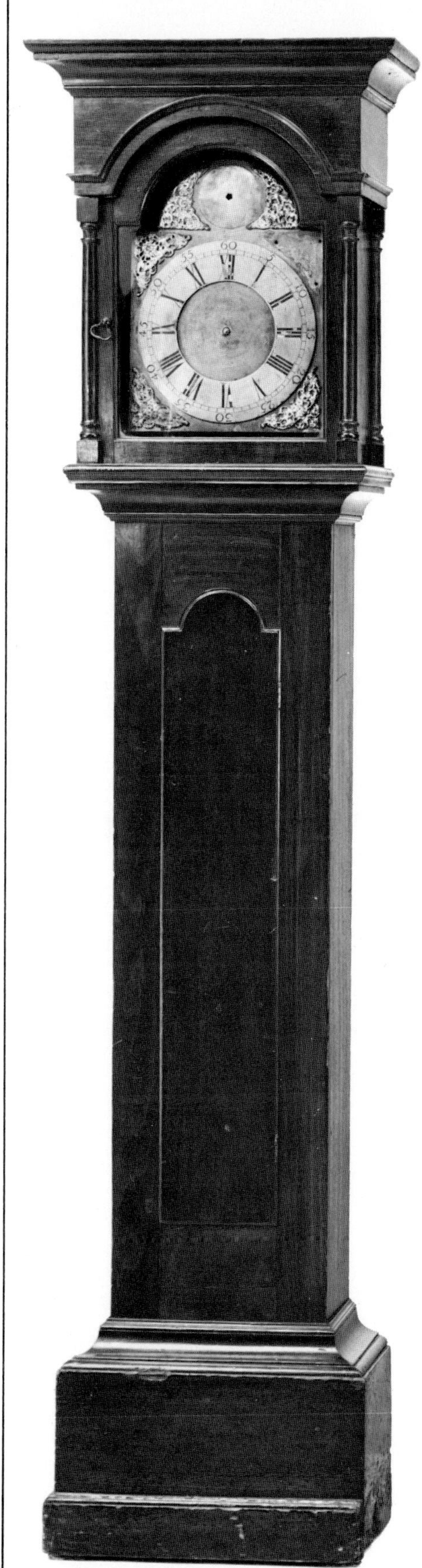

Detail of movement: Count wheel

tall clocks
MASSACHUSETTS

12

Massachusetts, 1780–1790
"Aaron Willard." painted on dial.

woods
Mahogany; base molding of hood, cherry; back of rear feet and back of hood, white pine.

dimensions
CASE: H. 91$\frac{1}{16}$ in. (231.3 cm); hood: W. 20$\frac{3}{8}$ in. (51.8 cm), FW. 15$\frac{5}{8}$ in. (39.8 cm), D. 10$\frac{1}{4}$ in. (26.1 cm); lower case: H. 59$\frac{3}{4}$ in. (151.8 cm), W. 18$\frac{7}{8}$ in. (47.9 cm), FW. 13$\frac{3}{4}$ in. (34.9 cm), D. 9$\frac{3}{4}$ in. (24.8 cm), FD. 7$\frac{1}{4}$ in. (18.4 cm).
DIAL: 17 in. (43.2 cm), W. 12$\frac{1}{16}$ in. (31.1 cm).
MOVEMENT: 6$\frac{7}{16}$ in. (16.4 cm), W. 4$\frac{1}{2}$ in. (11.5 cm), D. 2$\frac{1}{2}$ in. (6.4 cm).

inscription
Written in pencil on inside of lower case door near the top: "Oct. 20 1835/ J Green/ May 5 1837 / J. Green."

description
Hood with three brass spired ball finials on plinths, applied fretwork, cornice with an arch at center front, freestanding brass stop-fluted columns at the front corners of the hood, quarter columns at the rear, arched sidelights, and a glazed door with an arch at the center of the top. Waist with a cove molding at the top, brass stop-fluted quarter columns at the front corners, and a door with applied molding on the edges and an arched top. Base with a cove molding at the top and ogee bracket feet.

Painted iron dial with roman hour numerals, arabic minute numerals, floral sprays in the spandrels, transfer-printed global maps in front of the moon dial, seconds dial above the pierced hands and calendar aperture below.

Eight-day movement with brass plates and wheels, cut pinions, seconds pendulum with anchor-recoil escapement, grooved winding drums, two double-hung weights, rack and snail hourly striking system, bell hammer with a coil spring like a section of short, heavy watch spring instead of usual leaf spring, an alarm attachment on the time side with single-hung weight on pull chain, and a double-headed alarm hammer inside the bell.

condition
Finials replaced; fretwork repaired; escutcheon of hood door missing; case refinished. Minute hand replaced, and edges sharp and square in contrast to beveled edges of hour hand; calendar disc repainted; movement retains original polish.

provenance
Mrs. Clark McIlwaine, West Hartford, Conn., and Washington, D.C.

comments
The handsome case of this clock with its fretwork, arched cornice, and brass stop-fluted columns is typical of many tall clocks with works signed by Aaron Willard. The absence of inlay, the ogee bracket feet, and the arched door suggest this clock was made in the earlier part of Willard's career, perhaps when he worked in Grafton or Roxbury before his move to Boston in the 1790's. He probably was trained by his older brother, Benjamin, in Grafton and moved with Simon to Roxbury in 1780. The dial is mounted on the movement by extra long feet.

Gift of Mrs. Clark McIlwaine
1946.1

1946.1

Aaron Willard.
THE PACIFIC OCEAN
NORTH AMERICA
Great S. SEA
Barbary
AFRICA
TARTARY

tall clocks
MASSACHUSETTS

13

Boston, Massachusetts, about 1800
"Aaron Willard / Boston." painted on dial.

woods
Mahogany; backboard and top of hood, white pine; secondary wood in hood, spruce.

dimensions
CASE: H. 91 in. (231.1 cm); hood: W. 19⅝ in. (49.9 cm), FW. 14⅞ in. (37.8 cm), D, 9½ in. (24.2 cm), FD. 8¼ in. (21.0 cm); lower case: H. 60⅛ in. (152.7 cm), W. 18¹³⁄₁₆ in. (47.8 cm), FW. 13⁷⁄₁₆ in. (34.1 cm), D. 9¾ in. (24.8 cm), FD. 7¹⁄₁₆ in. (17.9 cm).
DIAL: H. 17¼ in. (43.8 cm), W. 12⅛ in. (30.8 cm).
MOVEMENT: H. 6½ in. (16.5 cm), W. 4½ in. (11.4 cm), D. 2½ in. (6.3 cm).

description
See No. 12. This clockcase is very similar except that it is veneered and inlaid.

Painted iron dial with roman hour numerals, arabic minute numerals, floral sprays in the spandrels and in the arch at the top of the dial, a seconds dial above pierced hands and a calendar aperture below.

Eight-day movement with brass plates and wheels, cut pinions, grooved winding drums, two double-hung weights, seconds pendulum with anchor-recoil escapement, and a rack and snail striking system.

condition
Fret restored on right side and repaired on left side; back of left rear foot at base and side of left front foot at base restored; case refinished. Paint on both main and calendar dials deeply reticulated; crutch wire very awkwardly repaired.

provenance
The Rev. Reuben Peaslee, Plaistow, N.H. (ca. 1840); Mrs. Mary A. Sawyer, Me.; Fred Wellington Ayer, Bangor, Me.; Francis P. Garvan, New York, N.Y.

bibliography
American Antiques in New England, Collection of Fred Wellington Ayer, Sale, New York, American Art Galleries, May 3–4, 1929, p. 49, no. 215 (illus.). Meyric R. Rogers, "Garvan Furniture at Yale," *The Connoisseur Year Book* 1960, p. 16, no. 18.

comments
Aaron Willard established his business in Boston just over the Roxbury line in the 1790's and ran it until his son, Aaron Jr., took over in 1823. This is one of Willard's signed Boston clocks; the veneered and inlaid case in the newer neoclassical style, suggests a somewhat later date than that of No. 12. Certainly clockmakers may have sold clock movements to customers who supplied the cases themselves, but it is apparent that very often clocks were finished in the clockmaker's shop. The Connecticut clockmaker Daniel Burnap, for instance, advertised for a journeyman to make fifteen or twenty clock cases in 1795 (see No. 5). At one time Aaron Willard was in partnership with the Boston cabinetmaker James Blake, who undoubtedly made many of the cases for Willard's Boston clocks. Their partnership was dissolved in November, 1804 (*Independent Chronicle,* XXVI, 2462, Nov. 1, 1804).

The Mabel Brady Garvan Collection
1930.2283

AARON WILLARD
BOSTON.

Ashby, Massachusetts, 1801–1820
"Alex. T. Willard. / Ashby." painted on dial.

woods
White pine; door and cove molding at top of waist, basswood.

dimensions
CASE: H. 85 in. (215.9 cm); hood: W. 20⅞ in. (53.0 cm), FW. 14½ in. (36.8 cm), D. 12⅝ in. (32.1 cm); lower case: H. 62¾ in. (159.4 cm), W. 16 in. (40.7 cm), FW. 12⅛ in. (30.8 cm), D. 9⅞ in. (25.1 cm), FD. 8⅛ in. (20.7 cm).
DIAL: H. 16¾ in. (42.6 cm), W. 12¼ in. (31.1 cm).
MOVEMENT: H. 8⅝ in. (21.9 cm), W. 7¼ in. (18.4 cm), D. 3⅜ in. (8.6 cm).

inscription
"67" written on back plate.

description
Hood with a flat molded top, freestanding bulbous turned columns at the front corners, and a door with an arched glass. Waist with a cove molding at the top and a door with an arched top. Base with a cove molding at the top, skirts cut with serpentine curves and French feet.

White painted wooden dial with black roman hour numerals, arabic minute numerals, painted roses in the spandrels and arch at the top, and pierced hands.

Thirty-hour movement with maple plates, separate weights on cords attached to one end of drum to drive time and strike trains, pull-wind by a separate cord, integral flange to separate running and winding cords, anchor-recoil escapement with brass wheel for seconds pendulum, and a count-wheel striking system.

condition
Case refinished; two top pillars restored on their outer ends; pendulum suspension beam replaced; count wheel repaired at lobe for striking two.

provenance
Frank MacCarthy, Longmeadow, Mass.; Francis P. Garvan, New York, N.Y.

comments
From 1790 to 1820 members of the Willard and Edwards families of Ashby, Massachusetts, produced many pine tall clocks with wooden works, and rosebuds painted on the dials (Laurence Luther Barber, "The Clockmakers of Ashby, Massachusetts," *Antiques*, 23 [May 1933], pp. 178–180). Alexander Tarbell Willard, whose signature is on this dial, was a third cousin of the famous clockmaker, Simon, of Roxbury. Alexander was born in Ashburnham, Massachusetts, in 1774, was probably apprenticed to Abraham Edwards, and moved to Ashby in 1801. This flat-topped pine case, like most of those on the Ashby clocks, is relatively simple, with the French feet and serpentine curved skirts the only real hints of fashionable taste.

The Mabel Brady Garvan Collection
1930.2327

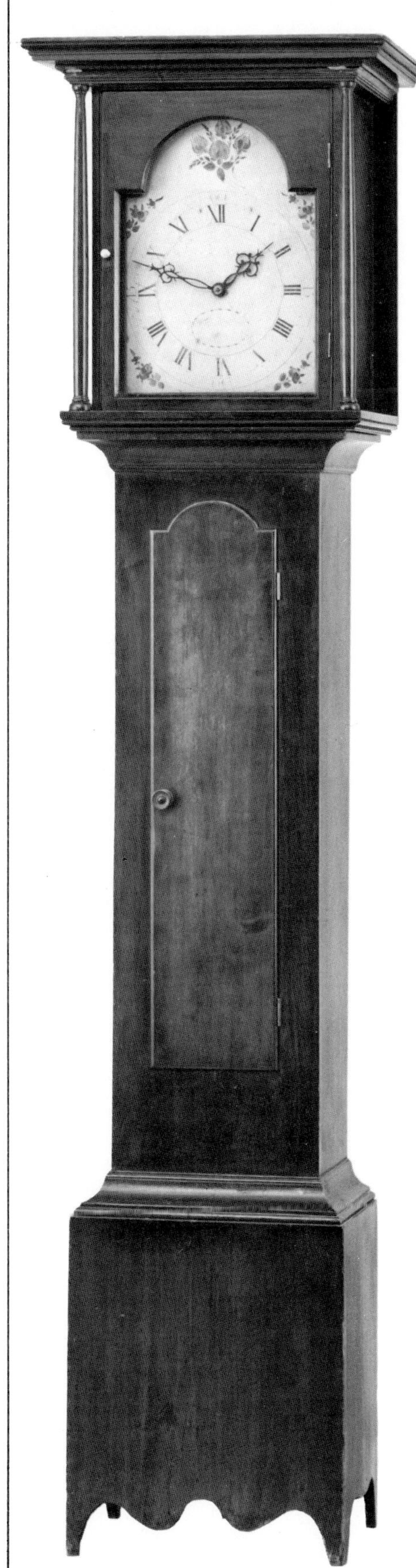

Detail of movement: Count wheel

tall clocks
MASSACHUSETTS

Newburyport, Massachusetts, 1800–1815
"DAVID WOOD / NEWBURYPORT" painted on dial.

woods
Mahogany; northern red pine.

dimensions
CASE: H. 89½ in. (227.3 cm); hood: W. 20½ in. (52.1 cm), D. 9½ in. (24.2 cm), FD. 9 in. (22.9 cm); lower case: H. 61⅛ in. (155.3 cm), W. 18¹⁵⁄₁₆ in. (48.1 cm), FW. 13⅝ in. (34.6 cm), D. 9 in. (22.9 cm), FD. 6⁵⁄₁₆ in. (16.0 cm).
DIAL: H. 18¾ in. (47.6 cm), W. 13 in. (33.0 cm).
MOVEMENT: H. 6⅜ in. (16.2 cm), W. 4½ in. (11.4 cm), D. 2⅝ in. (6.7 cm).

description
Hood with three brass spired ball finials, a swan neck pediment with brass rosettes, a frieze with an arch at center front, fluted Corinthian columns at the front corners, double serpentine molding at the rear corners, diamond-shaped sidelights, and a veneered glazed door with an arched top. Waist with a cove molding at the top, fluted quarter columns at the front corners, a veneered line-inlaid door with an arched top, and a lozenge-shaped inlay at the bottom of the front. Base with a cove and ovolo molding at the top, a veneered and inlaid front, shaped skirts, and French feet.

Painted iron dial with roman hour numerals, floral sprays in the spandrels and in the arch at the top of the dial, calendar dial above pierced hour and minute hands, and seconds dial below.

Eight-day movement with brass plates and wheels, cut pinions, seconds pendulum with anchor-recoil escapement, grooved drums, two double-hung weights, and rack and snail striking system.

condition
New corner blocks on rear feet; refinished in 1965; paint on dial eroded by washing and abraded near "VII"; calendar hand replaced.

provenance
Henry H. Taylor, Bridgeport, Conn.; Francis P. Garvan, New York, N.Y.

comments
David Wood, who set up a shop in Newburyport, Massachusetts, in 1792, is perhaps best known for his shelf clocks, but he advertised as late as 1824 that he made clocks of all kinds. The veneered and inlaid case of this clock could have been made in the 1790's, but the bold and colorful floral decoration on the dial, which may possibly be of American manufacture, and the design of the hands, typical of many northern English and Scottish clocks, suggest a nineteenth-century date. The soaring figure of the fine light mahogany veneer on the façade is broken only by the inlaid lozenge between the waist and base. Delicate colonnettes with gilded Corinthian capitals support the pediment capped with two poorly drawn scrolls. Another David Wood tall clock, once owned by the Newburyport merchant James Blood, is in the Essex Institute, Salem, Massachusetts. The individual touch of the maker is evident in such details as the rounded edges of the brass plates in the movement and the provision of thumb screws for attachment to the seat board.

The Mabel Brady Garvan Collection
1930.2340

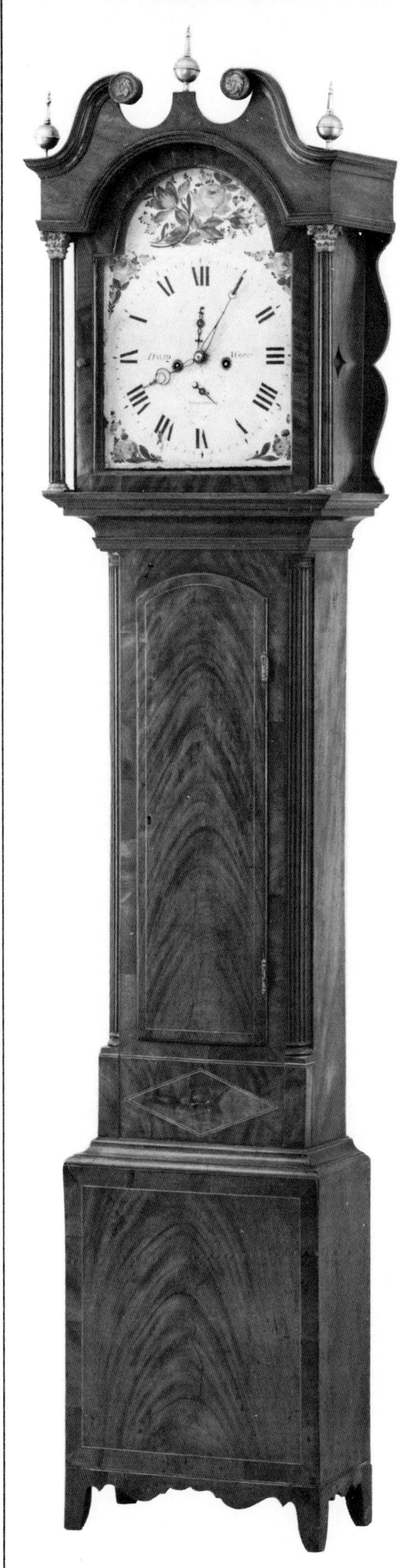

DAVID WOOD
NEWBURYPORT

tall clocks
MASSACHUSETTS

Massachusetts, about 1810 or possibly 1822

"Warranted by Kelley & Shepherd / Dartmouth / M^S" painted on dial.

woods
Mahogany; base molding on hood, cherry; top back of hood and secondary wood on door, white pine.

dimensions
CASE: H. 93¾ in. (238.1 cm); hood: W. 22 in. (55.9 cm), D. 10¼ in. (26.0 cm); lower case: H. 60¾ in. (154.3 cm), W. 20⁷⁄₁₆ (51.9 cm), FW. 15⅛ in. (38.4 cm), D. 9⅝ in. (24.4 cm), FD. 7 in. (17.8 cm).
DIAL: H. 18½ in. (47.0 cm), W. 13¹⁄₁₆ in. (33.2 cm).
MOVEMENT: H. 6¼ in. (15.8 cm), W. 4½ in. (11.4 cm), D. 2⅜ in. (6.1 cm).

description
Hood with three spired ball finials on diapered plinths, applied fretwork, cornice with an arch at center front, arched sidelights, spiral-turned columns at the front corners, and a glazed door with an arch at the top. Waist with a cove molding at the top, freestanding spiral turned columns and diaper-patterned blocks above and below the capitals and bases at the front corners.

Painted iron dial with roman hour numerals, arabic minute numerals, painted fruit and gilt arabesques in the spandrels, moon dial in the arch at the top flanked by transfer-printed global maps, seconds dial above the center of the main dial, day-of-the-month dial below, and pierced hour and minute hands.

Eight-day movement with brass plates, brass wheels, cut pinions, a seconds pendulum with anchor-recoil escapement, grooved drums, double-hung weights, and a rack and snail striking system.

condition
Fretwork repaired; feet missing.

provenance
Matthew Thacher (c. 1810); Harriet S. Thacher, Danvers, Mass.; Raymond L. Thacher, New Haven, Conn.; his wife Josephine Thacher, New Haven, Conn.

comments
Palmer lists both Nathaniel Shepherd and Ezra Kelley as being located in New Bedford, Massachusetts, although at some time they must have run a shop in Dartmouth, a town slightly to the southwest (*Am. Clocks*, pp. 226 and 275). About 1810 Nathaniel Shepherd was a partner with Kelley in selling watches, clocks, and clock oil. The family history stating that this clock was made for Matthew Thacher corroborates the date; however, a partially illegible inscription inside the lower case door reads "This clock was made in the summer/ of 1822 by Mr........" The dark mahogany case with its heavy rope turnings possibly supports this somewhat later date. The dial has many similarities to the one attributed to Nolen and Curtis on the clock by Frederick Wingate (No. 8) and may have been made by them or by one of their apprentices.

Gift of Josephine Thacher
1964.54.2

Warranted by Kelley & Shepherd
Dartmouth

tall clocks

NEW JERSEY

Elizabethtown, New Jersey, 1760–1779
"Aaron / Miller" engraved on dial.

woods
Cherry and red gum.

dimensions
CASE: H. 94 in. (238.8 cm); hood: W. 20 in. (50.7 cm), FW. 17 in. (43.2 cm), D. $10\frac{1}{8}$ in. (26.0 cm), FD. 9 in. (22.9 cm); lower case: H. $57\frac{1}{2}$ in. (146.0 cm), W. $16\frac{1}{8}$ in. (41.0 cm), FW. $12\frac{1}{4}$ in. (31.1 cm), D. $8\frac{13}{16}$ in. (22.4 cm), FD. $6\frac{3}{4}$ in. (17.1 cm).
DIAL: H. $15\frac{3}{4}$ in. (40.0 cm), W. $11\frac{1}{2}$ in. (29.2 cm).
MOVEMENT: H. $6\frac{7}{8}$ in. (17.5 cm), W. $4\frac{5}{8}$ in. (11.7 cm), D. $2\frac{1}{16}$ in. (5.2 cm).

description
Hood with three wooden ball finials on plinths, a cove- and ovolo-molded top, a frieze with an arch at center front, turned columns at the four corners, and a glazed door with an arched top. Waist with a cove molding at the top and a door with an arched top. Base with a cove molding at the top and straight bracket feet.

Wrought brass dial with roman hour numerals and arabic minute numerals on a silvered chapter ring, cast brass ornaments with masks and arabesques in the spandrels, cast dolphin ornaments flanking the signature plate in the arched top, stippled center, a seconds dial above the pierced hands and a calendar aperture below.

Eight-day movement with brass plates with the top right corner cut away and an arched opening at the base, brass wheels, cut pinions, seconds pendulum with anchor-recoil escapement, smooth winding drums, two double-hung weights, and a rack and snail repeating strike.

condition
Modern friction bushings; second hand replaced.

provenance
Descended in Edwards family; Charles Hoyt.

comments
According to its recorded history, this clock was handed down by inheritance in the family of Jonathan Edwards. However, it appears doubtful that Edwards, who lived for only a few months after he moved from Massachusetts to New Jersey in 1758 to be the president of Princeton, ever actually owned the clock. Other members of his family continued to live in New Jersey after his death, however, and one of them may have purchased it in the 1760's or the 1770's from Aaron Miller, who worked in Elizabethtown from about 1740 until his death in 1779. Miller often used tapered turned pillars to support the movement plates, and the hour hand is typical of his work. The baroque style ornaments in the spandrels would seem to suggest an earlier date than the one assigned to the clock. Nevertheless, Isaac Brokaw, Miller's son-in-law and heir (of his tools and trade), made a dial with identical ornaments as late as 1785 (Drost, p. 37). The remarkably well-preserved case of this clock has its original wooden ball finials and is made from red gum and cherry, popular woods with New Jersey cabinetmakers. Clocks with similar features are in the collection of Mr. and Mrs. Franklin Beaver of Allendale, New Jersey, and at Colonial Williamsburg.

Gift of Charles Hoyt
1950.76

Aaron
Miller
60
5
10
15
20
25
30
35
40
45
50
55
60
15
30
45
1

tall clocks

NEW JERSEY

18

Newark, New Jersey, 1760–1775
"Moses Ogden NEW=ARK" engraved on dial.

wood
Red gum.

dimensions
CASE: H. 82 1/16 in. (208.4 cm); hood: W. 18¾ in. (47.7 cm), FW. 16 in. (40.7 cm), D. 10⅜ in. (26.4 cm), FD. 9⅛ in. (23.2 cm); lower case: H. 58⅞ in. (149.5 cm), W. 18¾ in. (47.6 cm), FW. 13 7/16 in. (34.1 cm), D. 9¾ in. (24.8 cm), FD. 7 in. (17.8 cm).
DIAL: H. 15¾ in. (40.0 cm), W. 11½ in. (29.2 cm).
MOVEMENT: H. 6⅝ in. (16.8 cm), W. 4¾ in. (12.1 cm), D. 2⅝ in. (6.7 cm).

description
Hood with a flat cove-molded top, a frieze with an arch at center front, bulbous turned columns at the four corners, and a glazed door with an arched top. Waist with a cove molding at the top, and a door with an arched top. Base with an ogee molded top, a baseboard, and straight bracket feet.

Brass dial with roman hour numerals and arabic minute numerals, cast brass rococo ornaments in the lower spandrels and in the arched top on either side of the engraved moon dial; stippled center, seconds dial above pierced hands and calendar aperture below signature plate.

Eight-day movement with brass plates and wheels, cut pinions, bell bracket with ornamented end, plain pillars, two double-hung weights, a seconds pendulum with anchor-recoil escapement, wooden winding drums, and a rack and snail striking system.

condition
Left rear and both front blocks behind feet new; front feet new; upper right corner and right edge of case door restored; keyhole and area around lock patched; glass in hood door cracked; case refinished in 1964. Eyes in face at top of dial no longer move; two top spandrel ornaments missing; second hand probably replaced; modern bushings on upper train arbors; strike train fan arbor new, fan a crude replacement cut from sheet brass; drum on time side replaced; pendulum crutch repaired.

provenance
Francis P. Garvan, New York, N.Y.

comments
Generally clocks with arched dials have cases with arched or swan neck pediments, but some sophisticated clocks of the early eighteenth century and country clocks made as late as the nineteenth century have arched dials in flat-topped cases. The case of this clock by Moses Ogden of Newark, New Jersey, is identical to the case of a clock by Aaron Miller, who worked in neighboring Elizabethtown (Drost, illus. p. 171). The same cabinetmaker undoubtedly made them both. Movements by these two clockmakers also show similarities. Wooden winding drums and a thin sheet brass ratchet wheel fastened to the drum with nails are often used on clocks by Aaron Miller (see No. 17) and his heir Isaac Brokaw, which may suggest Ogden and Miller had common training. Other shared features are the form of the hour hand and the tapered turned movement pillars. The heavy cove and ogee moldings and bulbous columns at the front corners of the hood of No. 18 seem to belie a date in the mid-eighteenth century, when the rococo style was in full flower.

Moses Ogden was born in Newark in 1736 and probably began to work as a clockmaker just before his marriage to Mary Johnson of nearby Elizabethtown in 1759 (Drost, p. 190). Ogden, who died in 1814, appears to have been reasonably prosperous, and was referred to in 1780 as a merchant (Kenn Stryker-Rodda, "Jersey Rateables 1778–1780," *The Genealogical Magazine of New Jersey,* 44 [2], May 1969, p. 93). His interest in metalware went beyond clockmaking, for in 1768 an advertisement in the *New York Gazette and Weekly Mercury* indicates that he operated the Vesuvius Furnace at Newark, where "the moulding and casting of Iron Hollow Ware" was carried on. Later in 1773 he ran an air furnace in partnership with Edward and William Laight (*Extracts from American Newspapers Relating to New Jersey 1768–1769,* Vol. VII, p. 122, and Vol. X, pp. 100 and 101). The author knows of only one other clock by this maker, which may indicate that with his wide-ranging business interests Ogden actually devoted little time to clockmaking. The dial of this clock, engraved in the overarch with a moon or sun face with movable eyes, is perhaps one of the most humorous in the collection.

The Mabel Brady Garvan Collection
1930.2073

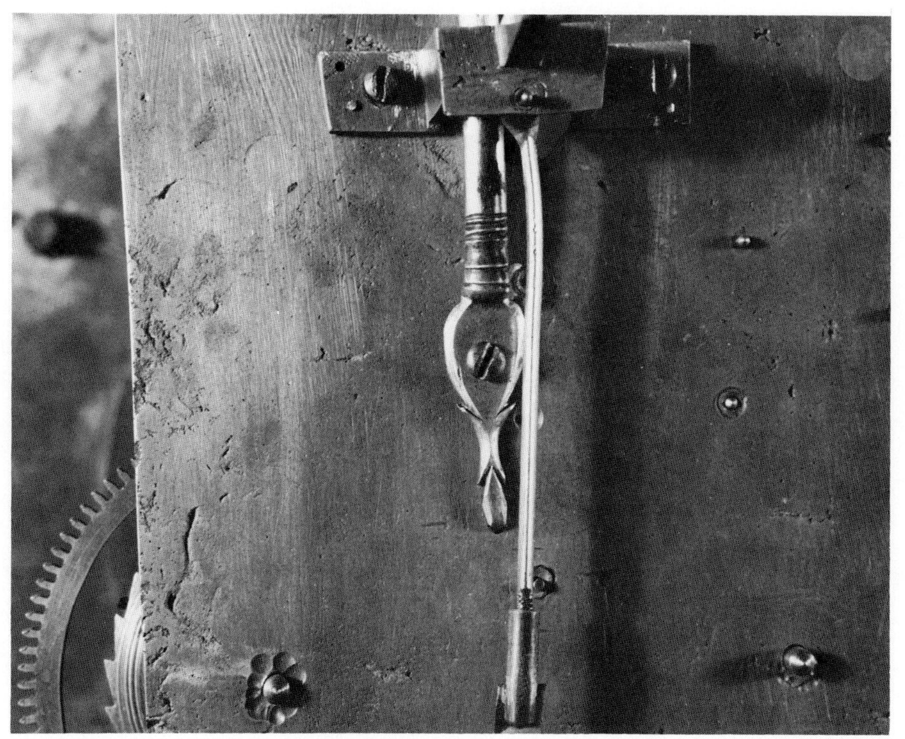

Detail of movement: Bell bracket

Moses Ogden New-Ark

19

Probably Mount Holly, New Jersey, about 1775
"William Hudson / MOUNT HOLLY " engraved on dial.

woods
American black walnut; backboard, sweet gum; back and top of hood, Southern white cedar; secondary wood in hood and glue-blocks, white pine.

dimensions
CASE: H. 97 9/16 in. (247.8 cm); hood: W. 21 3/4 in. (55.3 cm), FW. 18 7/8 in. (48.0 cm), D. 11 1/8 in. (28.3 cm), FD. 9 5/8 in. (24.5 cm); lower case: H. 65 7/16 in. (166.2 cm), W. 19 1/2 in. (49.5 cm), FW. 14 1/8 in. (35.9 cm), D. 10 1/4 in. (26.0 cm), FD. 7 5/8 in. (19.4 cm).
DIAL: H. 16 3/4 in. (42.5 cm), W. 12 in. (30.5 cm).
MOVEMENT: H. 6 1/2 in. (16.5 cm), W. 4 5/8 in. (11.7 cm), D. 2 5/8 in. (6.7 cm).

description
Hood with an urn and corkscrew finial, swan neck pediment with carved rosettes, a frieze with an arch at center front, bulbous turned columns at the front corners, and a glazed door with an arched top. Waist with a cove molding at the top, fluted quarter columns at the front corners, and a door with hollow upper corners. Base with an ogee molding at the top, fluted quarter columns at the front corners, molding with hollow upper corners applied to the front, and ogee bracket feet.

Wrought silvered brass dial with roman hour numerals and arabic minute and day-of-the-month numerals, engraved arabesques in the spandrels and above the winding holes, a seconds dial above the finely pierced hour and minute hands, and a moon dial in the arched top painted with stars on a blue ground.

Eight-day movement with brass plates, wide-rimmed brass wheels, cut pinions, a seconds pendulum with an anchor-recoil escapement, a rack and snail striking system, two double-hung weights, and smooth drums.

condition
Arched ends of board framing dial broken; case refinished; dial stained and mottled; large areas of silvering missing. Paint on moon dial abraded. Mechanism to operate moon and calendar dials missing; pivot holes defaced by punching to compensate for wear; calendar hand missing.

provenance
Francis P. Garvan, New York, N.Y.

comments
In the *Philadelphia Gazette* of February 10, 1773, Wood and Hudson of Mount Holly, New Jersey, advertised that they carried on a clockmaking business. Isaac Wood was most probably the Wood in the partnership. Mount Holly is not far from Philadelphia, and understandably the case reflects the urban Philadelphia style. The silvered dial, whose hemispheres flanking the moon dial have been engraved with floral motifs rather than the usual maps, must have at one time been quite handsome, although much of the silvering is now missing. Edward LaFond has observed that clocks by Hudson have heavily constructed movements with a peculiar striking system stop that arrests the striking system by means of a lever falling in the path of a pin located on the rim of the warning wheel. The celebrated English watch and clockmaker Robert Roskell of Liverpool also used this system. Good examples of Hudson's work are in the collections of Sewell C. Biggs, Middletown, Delaware, and Ronald Shireman of Hanover, Pennsylvania.

The Mabel Brady Garvan Collection
1930.2071

William Hudson
MOUNT HOLLY

20

New Jersey, 1800–1810

"ISAAC BROKAW, BRIDGE TOWN" painted on dial.

woods

Mahogany; bottom molding on hood, red gum; side of hood and glueblocks, white pine; backboard, bottom board, and top of clock, tulip.

dimensions

CASE: H. 95 13/16 in. (243.4 cm); hood: W. 19 3/8 in. (49.2 cm), FW. 18 1/2 in. (47.0 cm), D. 9 3/8 in. (23.8 cm), FD. 8 7/8 in. (22.6 cm); lower case: H. 63 1/4 in. (160.7 cm), W. 18 13/16 in. (47.8 cm), FW. 13 5/16 in. (33.8 cm), D. 9 9/16 in. (24.3 cm), FD. 6 7/8 in. (17.5 cm).
DIAL: H. 18 3/4 in. (47.6 cm), W. 13 in. (33.0 cm).
MOVEMENT: H. 6 9/16 in. (16.7 cm), W. 4 3/4 in. (12.1 cm), D. 2 11/16 in. (6.8 cm).

inscription

"OSBORNE" cast on secondary plate between dial and movement.

description

Hood with three brass spired ball finials on small plinths, swan neck pediment with inlaid terminals, a frieze with inlaid fluting at the corners and center above the arch, freestanding fluted columns at the front corners, and a glazed door with an arch at the top. Waist with a cove molding at the top, three bands of inlaid fluting, fluted quarter columns at the front corners, a door with an elliptical inlay and serpentine top, and an elliptical inlay within a rectangle at the bottom. Base with a cove molding at the top, a circular inlay on the front, serpentine curved skirts, and French feet.

Painted iron dial with roman hour numerals and arabic minute numerals, painted fans in the spandrels, a seconds dial above the pierced hands and a calendar aperture below, and transfer-printed global maps flanking the moon dial.

Eight-day movement with brass plates with an arch-shaped opening at the bottom, brass wheels, cut pinions, seconds pendulum with anchor-recoil escapement, smooth drums, two double-hung weights, and a count wheel striking system.

condition

Finials replaced; crack in front panel of base repaired; front left foot, parts of front right foot, and both rear feet restored; case refinished.

provenance

Alexander M. Hudnut, New York, N.Y., and Princeton, N.J.; Francis P. Garvan, New York, N.Y.

bibliography

Duncan Phyfe and Other Fine Early American Furniture and Decorations. Collection of Alexander M. Hudnut of Princeton, New Jersey, Sale, New York, American Art Association, November 19, 1927, p. 62, no. 81; Palmer, *Am. Clocks*, no. 47.

comments

Isaac Brokaw (1746–1826), an apprentice and son-in-law of Aaron Miller (see No. 17), worked first in Elizabethtown and after 1788–89 in Bridgetown, New Jersey, where he continued to make clocks until he turned the business over to his son Aaron in 1816 (Drost, pp. 16 and 27). In making his clocks, Brokaw continued to use the old-fashioned count wheel striking system many years after it was abandoned by other clockmakers. This clock with the dial inscribed "Bridgetown" is among the 125 tall clocks by him that are known. Its painted dial and neoclassical style case suggest a date late in the clockmaker's career. A case of similar design was labeled in 1807 by the cabinetmakers Abraham Rosett and Abraham M. Mulford of Elizabethtown (*Antiques*, 19, No. 3 [March, 1931], 232). On the Yale example an added feeling of height is gained from the effective use of circular and elliptical stringing and the vertical thrust of the fluted inlay, columns, and quarter columns.

The Mabel Brady Garvan Collection
1930.2095

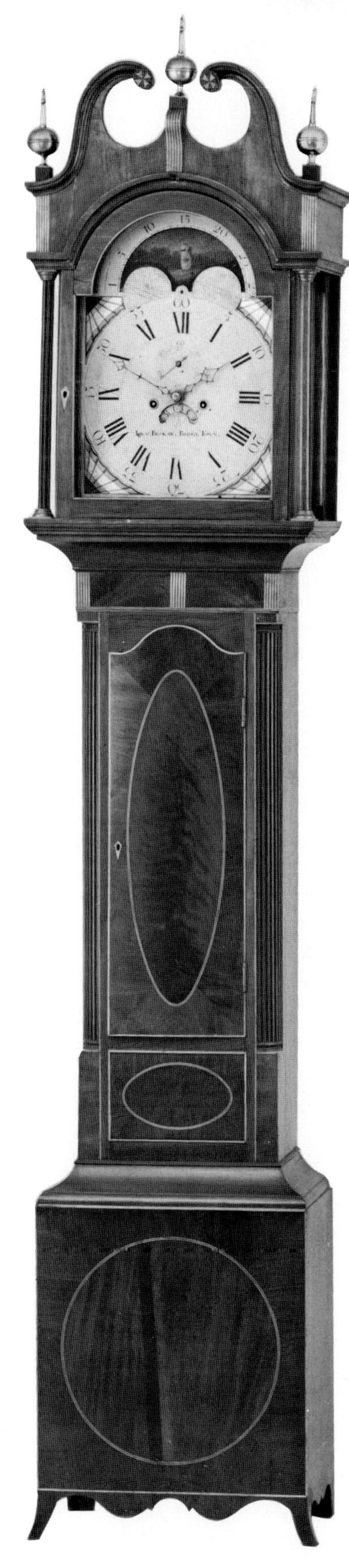

ISAAC BROKAW, BRIDGE TOWN.

tall clocks

NEW YORK

21

New York or New Jersey, 1790–1810

woods

Mahogany veneer; sides of hood and case, cherry; backboard, back of hood, and glueblocks, white pine; top of hood, tulip.

dimensions

CASE: H. 97⅛ in. (246.7 cm); hood: W. 20⅜ in. (51.8 cm), FW. 19 in. (48.3 cm), D. 10⅞ in. (27.7 cm), FD. 10¼ in. (26.1 cm); lower case: H. 64⅝ in. (164.1 cm), W. 18⅞ in. (47.9 cm), FW. 12¾ in. (32.4 cm), D. 10 in. (25.4 cm), FD. 6¹⁵⁄₁₆ in. (17.6 cm).
DIAL: H. 18¼ in (46.4 cm), W. 13 in. (33.0 cm).
MOVEMENT: H. 6¼ in. (16.0 cm), W. 5 in. (12.7 cm), D. 2⅝ in. (6.7 cm).

description

Hood with three spired urn finials, swan neck pediment with inlaid terminals, frieze with swags and bowknot inlaid and an arch at center front, freestanding fluted columns at the corners, oval sidelights, and a glazed door with an arch at the center. Waist with a cove molding at the top, fluted quarter columns at the front corners, and a door with a flatheaded arched top and a patera at the center. Base with a cove molding at the top, paneled front with inlaid paterae, and ogee bracket feet.

Painted iron dial with roman hour numerals, arabic minute numerals, oval medallions and arabesques in the spandrels, a seconds dial above the pierced hands and a calendar aperture below, transfer-printed global maps flanking the moon dial.

Eight-day movement with brass plates attached to the seat board with hook bolts at the bottom center of each (see also No. 30), brass wheels, cut pinions, seconds pendulum with anchor-recoil escapement, smooth drums, two double-hung weights, and a rack and snail striking system.

condition

New glass and new hinges on hood door; shrinkage crack in front panel of base repaired; case refinished. Dial virtually perfect for its age, a bit of paint flaked off over one dial foot; movement rebushed.

provenance

Alexander M. Hudnut, New York, N.Y., and Princeton, N.J.; Francis P. Garvan, New York, N.Y.

bibliography

Nutting, *Treasury*, no. 3268; *Collection of Alexander M. Hudnut*, p. 36, no. 58.

comments

The unsigned movement offers no immediate clue to the place of manufacture of this clock but the tall narrow proportions and attenuated scrolled pediment are characteristic features of many Federal period New York and New Jersey clocks. Other elements also point to the middle colonies: tulip and pine secondary woods are often found on New York and New Jersey furniture; the paterae on the door and base, and the shaded drops on the pediment are inlays preferred by cabinetmakers in those two areas (Montgomery, fig. 327).

The Mabel Brady Garvan Collection
1930.2126

15
10
20
5
25
1
29
60
55
5
50
10
45
15
40
20
35
25
30
60
50
10
40
20
30
21
24
27
31
15

tall clocks

NEW YORK

22

Albany, New York, 1800–1805

"BASSETT & WARFORD / ALBANY" painted on dial.

woods

Mahogany; inner base molding on hood, cherry.

dimensions

CASE: H. 93 in. (236.2 cm), MH. 95½ in. (242.6 cm); hood: W. 19⅞ in. (50.5 cm), FW. 18⅝ in. (47.3 cm), D. 10⅛ in. (25.7 cm), FD. 9⅝ in. (24.5 cm); lower case: H. 66 in. (167.6 cm), W. 19⅛ in. (48.6 cm), FW. 13⅝ in. (34.6 cm), D. 9⅝ in. (24.4 cm), FD. 6⅞ in. (17.5 cm).
DIAL: H. 16½ in. (41.9 cm), W. 12 in. (30.5 cm).
MOVEMENT: H. 6 11/16 in. (17.0 cm), W. 5 1/16 in. (12.8 cm), D. 2 11/16 in. (6.9 cm).

inscription

"Osborne's / MANUFACTORY / BIRMINGHAM" cast in secondary plate between dial and movement.

description

Hood with a swan neck pediment with inlaid terminals, a frieze with inlaid fluting at the corners and at the center above an arch with an inlaid keystone, freestanding fluted columns at the front corners, reeded molding at the rear corners, arched sidelights, and a glazed door with an arched top. Waist with a cove molding at the top, three bands of inlay, fluted quarter columns at the front corners, pointed elliptical inlay below the columns, and a door with a serpentine top, an elliptical inlay, and quarter paterae near the bottom. Base with a cove molding at the top, circular inlay on the front, quarter paterae in the corners, and straight bracket feet.

Painted iron dial with roman hour numerals, arabic minute numerals, gilt medallions, arabesques and swags in the spandrels and in the arch at the top, seconds dial above the pierced hands and calendar aperture below.

Eight-day movement with brass plates with arched openings at the bottom, brass wheels, cut pinions, seconds pendulum with anchor-recoil escapement, grooved drums, two double-hung weights, and a rack and snail striking system.

condition

Finials missing; wood around hinges repaired; case refinished in 1963; paint on main dial chipped over dial feet; calendar dial renumbered in ink; second hand replaced; plywood seat board; one lever in the striking mechanism crudely repaired.

provenance

Henry H. Taylor, Bridgeport, Conn.; Francis P. Garvan, New York, N.Y.

comments

The dial of this clock is painted with the names "Bassett & Warford," for the Albany, New York, silversmiths Nehemiah B. Bassett and Joseph Warford, who were in partnership between August 25, 1800, and October 7, 1805 (Norman S. Rice and James H. Halpin, "Joseph Warford, Silversmith of Albany and Salem, New York," *Antiques,* 85 [April 1964], 429–430). The tall, beautifully inlaid case is typical of some of the finest New York clock cases in the neoclassical period. A very similar clock signed only by Bassett is in the Albany Institute of History and Art (Rice, *New York Furniture Before 1840,* p. 52).

The Mabel Brady Garvan Collection
1930.2018

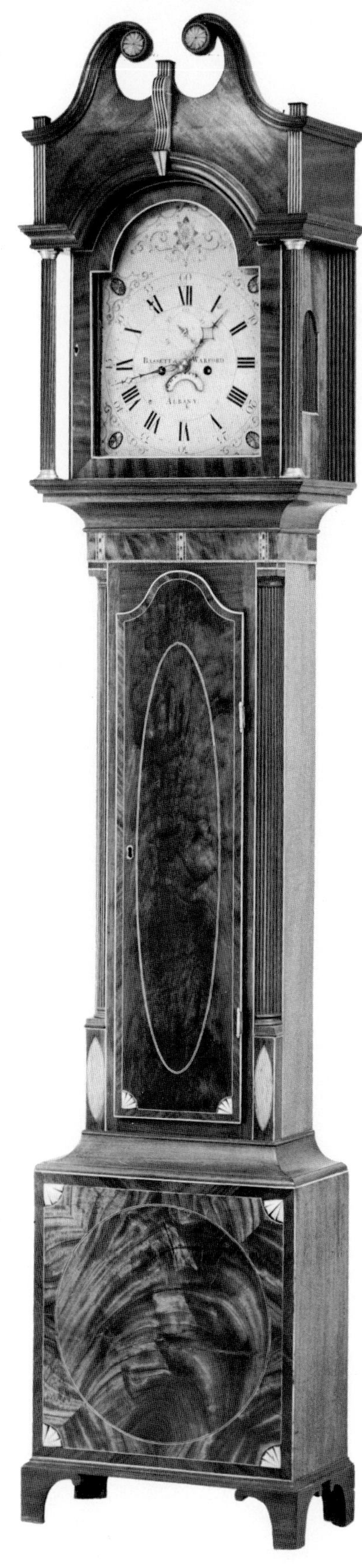
WARFORD
ALBANY

HEINE

BASSETT & WARFORD
ALBANY.

tall clocks

PENNSYLVANIA

23

Philadelphia, Pennsylvania, 1725–1740
"Jos Wills Philadelphia" engraved on dial.

woods
Pine of the *Taeda* group; molding on base of hood, cove molding on top of waist, and door of hood, ash; top of hood, white pine.

dimensions
CASE: H. 79¼ in. (201.3 cm); hood: W. 22½ in. (57.2 cm), FW. 16⅞ in. (42.9 cm), D. 14¼ in. (36.2 cm), FD. 11¼ in. (28.6 cm); lower case: H. 58¹¹⁄₁₆ in. (149.1 cm), W. 18⁵⁄₁₆ in. (46.5 cm), FW. 12⅜ in. (31.4 cm), D. 12¼ in. (31.1 cm), FD. 9 in. (22.9 cm).
DIAL: H. 10⅞ in. (27.6 cm), W. 10⅞ in. (27.6 cm).
MOVEMENT: H. 5⅞ in. (14.6 cm), W. 6 in. (15.3 cm), D. 4³⁄₁₆ in. (10.7 cm).

description
Hood with a flat molded cornice, turned half columns at the four corners, rectangular side-lights, and a glazed door. Waist with a cove molding at the top and a door with a glazed oval peephole. Base with cove and ovolo moldings at the top, an ogee and ovolo molding above the baseboard with a half-round molding near the bottom above very short straight bracket feet.

Square wrought brass dial of thin metal with roman hour numerals, arabic minute numerals, cast bronze amorini and crowns in the spandrels, engraved fleur-de-lis between the hour numerals and at the corners, stippled center, pierced hands, and a silvered calendar dial below the signature plate.

Thirty-hour movement with rectangular iron corner posts, brass top and bottom plates, three auxiliary brass pillars to support time and strike trains arranged front to back, brass wheels, cut pinions, seconds pendulum with anchor-recoil escapement, one weight on iron chain over spiked wooden drums to drive both trains, and a count wheel strike on the inside of bell.

condition
Four new corner blocks in base; knob missing from door; fastener on door not original. Center post has been broken and repaired; two screws and dial washer replaced; bell cracked.

provenance
Harry Arons, Ansonia, Conn.; Henry H. Taylor, Bridgeport, Conn.; Francis P. Garvan, New York, N.Y.

comments
The Philadelphia clockmaker Joseph Wills was working as early as 1725. The stylistic characteristics of his tall clock illustrated here suggest that it was made early in his career, and, moreover, that it may be the earliest tall clock represented in the Yale collections. The case, which is made of pine stained a dark brown, is short, and has a bold projecting architecturally molded cornice, a peephole just below the center of the waist door, and a broad, squat base. The dial presents a rich appearance and reflects the William and Mary style in the spandrel ornaments of amorini supporting crowns, intricately pierced hands, and stippled center. The construction of the movement with four iron corner posts is unusual on American clocks. The clocks made later in Wills's career (he died in 1759) are sometimes housed in elaborate rococo style cases (*Antiques*, Feb. 1931, pp. 96–97).

The Mabel Brady Garvan Collection
1930.2282

1930.2282
1930.2282

1980.2282

Jos Wills Philadelphia

tall clocks
PENNSYLVANIA

24

Pennsylvania, 1765–1775

woods
Walnut; backboard, red oak; top of hood, tulip.

dimensions
CASE: H. 92⅝ in. (235.3 cm); hood: W. 17$\frac{11}{16}$ in. (44.9 cm), FW. 15¾ in. (40.0 cm), D. 10⅝ in. (27.0 cm), FD. 9½ in. (24.2 cm); lower case: H. 71⅝ in. (181.9 cm), W. 16¾ in. (42.5 cm), FW. 11$\frac{11}{16}$ in. (29.7 cm), D. 10¼ in. (26.0 cm), FD. 7¼ in. (18.4 cm).
DIAL: H. 10⅝ in. (27.0 cm), W. 10⅝ in. (27.0 cm).
MOVEMENT: H. 5½ in. (14.0 cm), W. 5½ in. (14.0 cm), D. 2 in. (5.1 cm).

description
Hood with a flat molded cornice and a glazed door with "rattail" hinges. Waist with a cover molding on the top and a door with a glazed round peephole and "rattail" hinges. Plain base with an ogee molding at the top.

Square iron dial painted red, with roman hour numerals and arabic minute numerals engraved on a pewter chapter ring, gilded pewter ornaments of shells and C-scrolls in the spandrels, brass hour hand and iron minute hand.

Thirty-hour movement with square iron plates, original brass bushings, brass wheels, lantern pinions with one side open, strike train on right, time train on left, anchor-recoil escapement for loop-suspended seconds pendulum, pull-wind possibly for two weights (as the pulleys with sharp spikes for ropes have their own separate ratchets), two arms near top of backplate to attach movement to backboard, square spikes near bottom of backplate to steady movement, and rack and snail repeating strike.

condition
New corner blocks and braces in base; piece missing from lower left edge of case door; piece sawn out of center back; new piece at top of backboard; case refinished in 1964.

provenance
H. C. Taylor, Kennebunk, Me.; Francis P. Garvan, New York, N.Y. (1929).

comments
With its circular glazed peephole, square brass dial, quatrefoil wrought iron backplates on the door latches, flat cornice and narrow waist, this clock possesses all the earmarks of early eighteenth-century design; however, the gilded pewter ornaments in the spandrels are in a later, rococo style. The dial is unsigned, but the movement, dial, and hands are almost identical to early examples by George Hoff of Lancaster, Pennsylvania, who came to America from Germany in 1765. Hoff often used different metals for hour and minute hands—a brass hour hand with an iron minute hand, for example. The movement in No. 24, with lantern pinions typical of the German tradition in clockmaking, is hung from the backboard by projecting brackets on the backplate. Below are two spikes to steady the movement, particularly during winding. The walnut case with tulip as a secondary wood, and the large wrought iron hinges with splayed ends also suggest Pennsylvania as the place of origin. Two features of the case are unusual: the cove molding at the top of the waist is at an angle, and the door is hinged on the left rather than on the right side.

The Mabel Brady Garvan Collection
1930.2332

25

Pennsylvania, 1740–1760
"Jacob Godschalk Towamencin" engraved on dial.

woods
American black walnut; backboard, tulip.

dimensions
CASE: MH. center back: 94¾ in. (240.7 cm); hood: W. 19¼ in. (48.9 cm), FW. 16$\frac{7}{16}$ in. (41.8 cm), D. 11⅞ in. (30.2 cm), FD. 10½ in (26.7 cm); lower case: H. 68⅞ in. (174.9 cm), W. 16⅝ in. (42.2 cm), FW. 13 in. (33.0 cm), D. 10½ in. (26.7 cm), FD. 8$\frac{11}{16}$ in. (22.1 cm).
DIAL: H. 11 in. (27.9 cm), W. 11 in. (27.9 cm).
MOVEMENT: H. 6¼ in. (15.9 cm), W. 5$\frac{1}{16}$ in. (12.9 cm), D. 2$\frac{9}{16}$ in. (6.5 cm).

description
Hood with a domed top, two spired ball finials on fluted plinths, plain frieze, bulbous turned columns at the four corners, arched sidelights, and a glazed door. Waist with a cove molding at the top, and a door with a shell-carved top. Base with a cove molding at the top, a fielded panel at the front, and ogee bracket feet.

Square wrought brass dial with roman hour numerals and arabic minute numerals engraved on a silvered chapter ring, cast brass ornaments of amorini and crowns in the spandrels, compass rose engraving at the center, pierced hands, and a calendar aperture below the signature plate.

Thirty-hour movement with brass plates with arched openings at the base of both plates and arched upper corners on the backplate, brass wheels, cut pinions, seconds pendulum with anchor-recoil escapement, brass pull-winding chain over thin metal sprockets, a wooden pulley for the single weight, striking train on the right, time train on the left, rack and snail repeating strike.

condition
Domed pediment, finials, and possibly fluted plinths replaced; additional corner blocks; new bottom board in lower case; feet pierced; case refinished. Cast brass spandrels perhaps not original since there is a second set of holes beneath them, although it is possible that the second set of holes was drilled in error; upper trains fitted with modern bushings.

provenance
Howard Reifsnyder, Philadelphia, Pa.; Francis P. Garvan, New York, N.Y.

bibliography
Colonial Furniture, the Superb Collection of the Late Howard Reifsnyder, Sale, New York, American Art Galleries, April 24–27, 1929, p. 94, no. 385; Edgar C. Miller, Jr., *American Antique Furniture* (Baltimore: Lord Baltimore Press, 1937), II, p. 911 (illus. p. 913, no. 1801).

comments
"Towamencin" (township) engraved on the dial of this clock indicates a date of manufacture prior to 1763 or 1764, for at this time Jacob Godschalk, who had worked in the township from the 1720's, moved to Philadelphia. There until his death in 1782 he continued to practice his trade; as late as 1781 he received ten pounds "specie" to repair the state house clock (*Antiques,* 12 [Sept. 1927], p. 232). This movement is an unusually fine example of Godschalk's workmanship, for his clocks were often very crudely made and finished. The amorini and crown ornaments in the spandrels (like those on No. 23), the compass rose engraved center of the dial, the fielded panel, and the carved shell are decorative motifs commonly used in the mid-eighteenth century. Dials with compass-rose decorations are typical of Pennsylvania clockmakers working in the Schuylkill River Valley from Reading to Philadelphia. Some cases of Godschalk's Towamencin clocks are very sophisticated, such as the example in the Taradash Collection with an elaborate rococo style case (*Antiques,* 49–50 [Dec. 1946], p. 394). But the cabinetwork of this clock, with its poorly executed shell and unacademic bulbous columns on the hood, is provincial.

The Mabel Brady Garvan Collection
1930.2035

Jacob Godschalk Towamencin
60
5
10
15
20
25
30
35
40
45
50
55
16

Pennsylvania, 1765–1775
"B, Rittenhouse; Worcester." engraved on dial.

woods
American black walnut; top of hood, southeastern white cedar; backboard, tulip; bottom board, white oak; glueblock on left rear foot, white pine.

dimensions
CASE: MH. center back: 84¾ in. (215.3 cm); hood: W. 18⅜ in. (46.7 cm), FW. 11⅞ in. (30.2 cm), D. 10⅞ in. (27.7 cm), FD. 9⅞ in. (25.7 cm); lower case: H. 61 5/16 in. (155.7 cm), W. 16⅝ in. (42.2 cm), FW. 11⅞ in. (30.2 cm), D. 10⅝ in. (27.0 cm), FD. 7¾ in. (19.7 cm).
DIAL: H. 10 9/16 in. (26.8 cm), W. 10 9/16 in. (26.8 cm).
MOVEMENT: H. 6¼ in. (15.9 cm), W. 4½ in. (11.5 cm), D. 2½ in. (6.4 cm).

description
Hood with a cove and ovolo molded top, plain frieze, turned columns applied to front corners, quarter columns at the rear corners, and a glazed door. Waist with a cove molding at the top and a door with quarter-round molded edges. Base with a cove molding at the top and straight bracket feet.

Square wrought brass dial with roman hour numerals and arabic minute numerals engraved on a silvered brass chapter ring, cast brass ornaments of flower urns and arabesques in the spandrels, engraved leaves at the center, and pierced hands.

Thirty-hour movement with brass plates with an arched opening at the bottom, deep-rimmed brass wheels, cut pinions, strike train on the right, time train on the left, seconds pendulum with anchor-recoil escapement, iron pull chain for winding, single weight drive with winding ratchet on strike train only, and a rack and snail strike.

condition
Vertical crack at front of base; lower edge of door missing; corner block under right front foot missing. Time train holes rebushed.

provenance
Walter B. Sheppard, Denver, Col.

comments
The ovolo- and cove-molded pediment of this clock and its square brass dial with flower and urn ornaments in the spandrels ordinarily would prompt a dating prior to 1750, but other evidence suggests the clock was made later in the eighteenth century. The engraved center of the dial is in the rococo style, and the maker, Benjamin Rittenhouse, would not have completed his apprenticeship before 1761. Less renowned than his older brother David, Benjamin was probably trained by him as a clock and instrument maker. "Worcester" inscribed on the dial is the name of the town next to Norristown where the brothers were born. Benjamin apparently continued to work and live in Worcester until the first decade of the nineteenth century, when he is listed in the Philadelphia *Directories* as an instrument maker.

Bequest of Walter B. Sheppard
1950.64

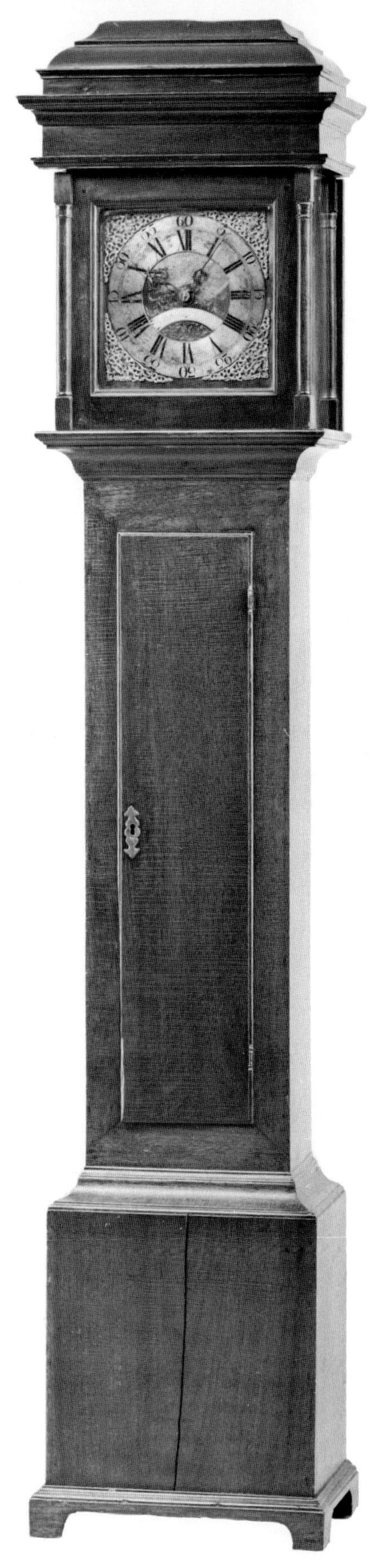

B. Rittenhouse: Worcester

Philadelphia, Pennsylvania, 1760–1790
"JN.O WOOD PHILADELPHIA" painted on dial.

woods
American black walnut; top of hood, white pine.

dimensions
CASE: H. 95 5/16 in. (242.1 cm); hood: W. 23 3/8 in. (59.4 cm), FW. 20 1/2 in. (52.1 cm), D. 10 7/8 in. (27.7 cm), FD. 9 9/16 in. (24.3 cm); lower case: H. 64 1/8 in. (162.9 cm), W. 21 in. (53.3 cm), FW. 13 15/16 in. (35.4 cm), D. 11 3/8 in. (28.9 cm), FD. 7 9/16 in. (19.2 cm).
DIAL: H. 18 7/8 in. (40.8 cm), W. 13 in. (30.3 cm).
MOVEMENT: H. 6 in. (15.2 cm), W. 4 5/8 in. (11.8 cm), D. 2 5/8 in. (6.7 cm).

description
Hood with three urn-and-flame finials—the outer two on fluted plinths—swan neck pediment with dentilling and carved rosettes, frieze with a reeded keystone and an arch at center front, freestanding fluted columns at the front corners, turned balusters at the rear corners, arched sidelights, and a glazed door with an arched top. Waist with a cove molding at the top, applied molding on the rear corners, fluted quarter columns on the front corners, and a door with an arch and serpentine curves on the top. Base with a cove molding at the top, fluted quarter columns on the front corners, an applied panel with hollow corners, and ogee bracket feet.

Painted iron dial with roman hour numerals, arabic minute numerals, floral sprays in the spandrels, transfer-printed maps in front of the moon dial, seconds dial above the pierced hands and calendar aperture below.

Eight-day movement with extra heavy brass plates with rounded edges, brass wheels, cut pinions, seconds pendulum with anchor-recoil escapement, grooved drums, two double-hung weights, and a rack and snail striking system.

condition
Two finials restored; new plinths; glass cracked on right side of hood; molding of pediment at left corner restored; right rear foot restored; corner blocks replaced; cove molding below hood on right side restored. Paint on dial abraded; iron and steel parts extensively rusted and pitted.

provenance
Jacob Margolis, New York, N.Y.; Francis P. Garvan, New York, N.Y. (1929).

comments
The case of this clock is not exceptionally elaborate, but it has many fine points of Philadelphia cabinetwork: the richly figured wood was carefully chosen; fluted columns are set into the front corners; the finials are urn-and-flame shaped. This clock made by John Wood, Jr., is one of a number of clocks that have survived from the flourishing trade that he and his father conducted. In 1760, John Wood, Jr. (1736–1793) inherited the business on the corner of Front and Chestnut streets in Philadelphia from his father, who in his day had purchased engraved clock faces from the silversmith Joseph Richardson (William MacPherson Horner, Jr., *Blue Book of Philadelphia Furniture,* Philadelphia, 1935, p. 55). The son advertised extensively from 1760 to 1793 in both the English and German newspapers, stating that he sold clocks and watches and clock parts to the country trade. By the time he succumbed to yellow fever in 1793, he had accumulated a large fortune (*Penn. Mag. of History and Biography,* 56 (1932), p. 228). A particularly unusual feature of this case is the application of molding to the back edge of the waist section as well as to the sides and front.

The Mabel Brady Garvan Collection
1930.2200

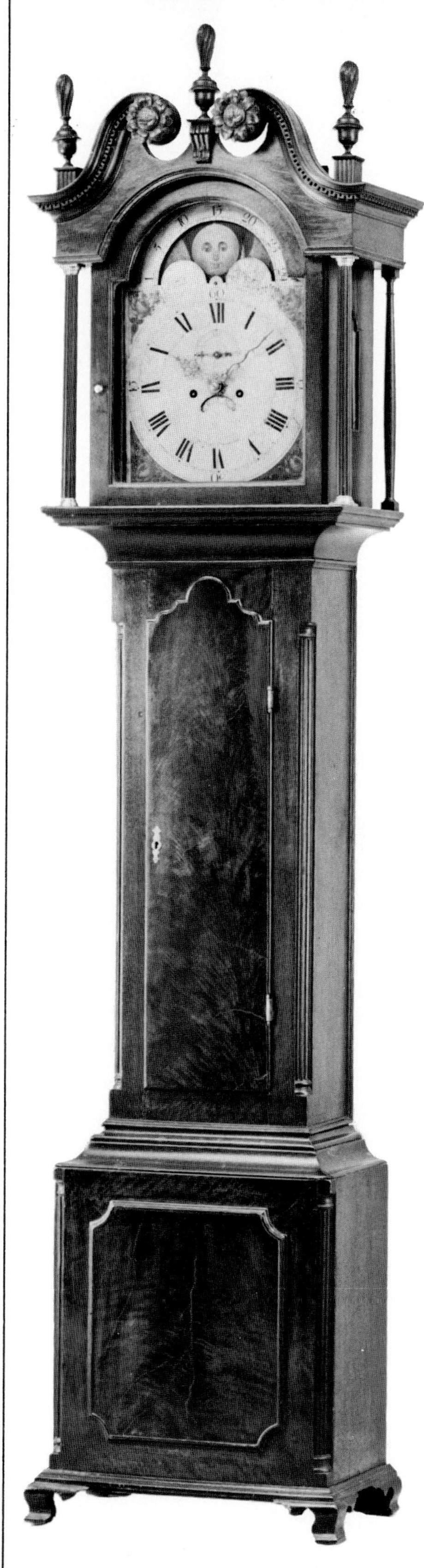

Jno Wood Philadelphia

28

Philadelphia, Pennsylvania, 1785–1795
"Griffith. Owen." painted on dial.

woods
American black walnut; secondary wood in hood and backboard, tulip.

dimensions
CASE: H. 96⅞ in. (246.1 cm); hood: W. 23⅞ in. (60.7 cm), FW. 20⅛ in. (51.1 cm), D. 12⅝ in. (32.1 cm), FD. 10⅞ in. (27.7 cm); lower case: H. 63¼ in. (160.7 cm). W. 21⅛ in. (53.7 cm), FW. 13½ in. (34.3 cm), D. 11⅛ in. (28.3 cm), FD. 7¼ in. (18.4 cm). *DIAL:* H. 18⅜ in. (46.7 cm), W. 13 in. (33.0 cm). *MOVEMENT:* H. 6½ in. (16.5 cm), W. 5⅛ in. (13.0 cm), D. 2¾ in. (7.0 cm).

inscription
"Wilson" cast in dial skeleton plate.

description
Hood with two urn bulb-and-flame finials on fluted plinths, a central petaled urn-and-flame finial, swan neck pediment with dentilling and carved rosettes, frieze with a keystone and arch at center front, freestanding turned balusters at the four corners, vase- and diamond-shaped sidelights, and a glazed door with an arched top. Waist with an ogee molding at the top, a thin band of applied molding, fluted quarter columns at the front corners, and a door with an arched and serpentine curved top. Base with an ogee molding at the top, an applied panel outlined with serpentine curves and double arches, fluted quarter columns at the front corners, and ogee bracket feet.

Painted iron dial with roman hour numerals, arabic minute and day-of-the-month numerals, painted floral sprays in the lower spandrels, painted strawberries in the upper spandrels, transfer-printed global maps in front of the moon dial, and pierced hour, minute, and calendar hands.

Eight-day movement with brass plates and wheels, cut pinions except for an open-sided lantern pinion in the dial train; gear with two diametrically opposite arms located between moon and calendar wheels advances moon and calendar dials simultaneously; hook bolts to attach movement to seatboard, seconds pendulum with anchor-recoil escapement, grooved drums, two double-hung weights, and a rack and snail striking system.

condition
Upper hinge of hood door replaced; new glass in sidelights; rear corner blocks replaced; waist door refinished. Paint on dial deeply reticulated and slightly abraded, some loss of details, particularly on maps; hour hand broken and crudely repaired; second hand replaced; movement shows considerable wear.

provenance
Francis P. Garvan, New York, N.Y.

bibliography
"American Furniture . . . ," *Handbook of the Gallery of Fine Arts* (Associates in Fine Arts at Yale University), 5 (1931), 58 (illus.).

comments
The cabinetmaker who fashioned the case of this clock freely interpreted the Philadelphia rococo style. All the decorative elements are very attenuated. Thin colonnettes, poised at the extreme edges of the hood, support a pediment crowned by unorthodox urn-and-flame finials. The fluted quarter columns are narrower than usual, and the applied panel on the base has a complex curved outline. The clock movement was made by Griffith Owen of Philadelphia. Owen, who began his apprenticeship with the Philadelphia clockmaker Jacob Godschalk in 1773, perhaps began to work on his own by 1780 ("Record of Servants and Apprentices Bound and Assigned Before Hon. John Gibson, Mayor of Philadelphia Dec. 5, 1772–May 21, 1773," *The Pennsylvania Magazine of History and Biography,* 34 [1910], p. 119). Godschalk died in 1781, and in 1782 Owen took over his master's task of caring for the state house clock (*Antiques,* 12 [September, 1927], p. 232). The movement of the Yale clock is made with an open-sided lantern pinion in the dial train. Owen was one of the few American clockmakers to use lantern pinions typical of the German tradition in clockmaking rather than the cut pinions of the English and French. He undoubtedly learned this technique from his German master, Godschalk, although the Godschalk clock in this collection is made with cut pinions (No. 25). Owen was listed in the Philadelphia *Directories* as late as 1814, and a number of his tall clocks are known (Palmer, *Am. Clocks,* 253).

The Mabel Brady Garvan Collection
1930.2326

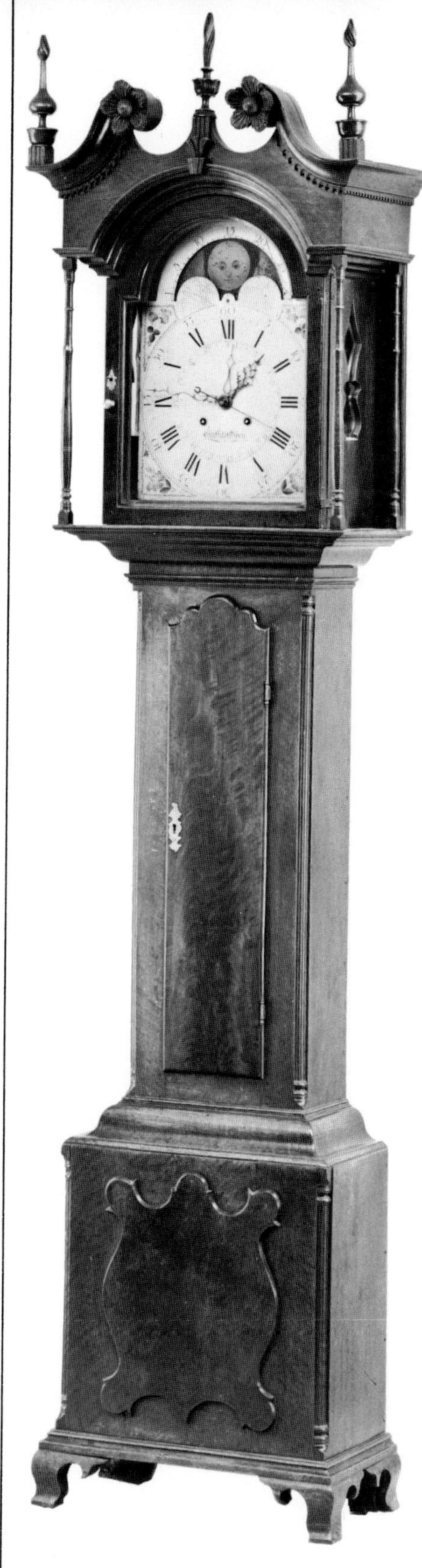

Griffith Owen

Yorktown, Pennsylvania, 1790
"John Fisher York Town" engraved on dial.

woods
American black walnut; top of hood, tulip.

dimensions
CASE: H. 100¾ in. (255.9 cm); hood: W. 24⅞ in. (63.2 cm), FW. 21⅜ in. (54.3 cm), D. 11¾ in. (29.9 cm), FD. 10¼ in. (26.1 cm); lower case: H. 67 in. (170.2 cm), W. 21⁵⁄₁₆ in. (54.1 cm), FW. 15³⁄₁₆ in. (38.6 cm), D. 10⅝ in. (27.0 cm), FD. 7½ in. (19.0 cm).
DIAL: D. 14½ in. (36.8 cm).
MOVEMENT: H. 6½ in. (16.5 cm), W. 5 in. (12.7 cm), D. 2¾ in. (7.0 cm).

description
Hood with three spired urn finials, swan neck pediment, fluted columns at the front corners, plain columns at the rear corners, oval sidelights, and a door with a circular glass. Waist with a cove molding at the top and a door with serpentine curves at the top. Base with a cove molding at the top, an applied panel at the front, and straight bracket feet.

Round wrought brass dial with roman hour numerals above the center of the dial, arabic minute numerals, months and days of the year, signs of the zodiac and of the seven "planets" of the pre-Copernican system engraved around the circumference, hour hand of fleur-de-lis shape, plain day-of-the-year hand, pierced and dart-shaped minute hand, pierced and counterbalanced second hand, astronomical dial below the center of the main dial with a moon face and stars on a revolving blued-steel dial, a planispheric map of the northern hemisphere, a stationary circle engraved with two counterclockwise series of roman numerals from one to twelve, and a deflected strip to indicate the hours of sunrise and sunset.

A thirty-five-day movement with brass plates with round headed arches at the bottom, flat-headed arches on the sides, and projections at the top to support a pallet arbor; brass wheels, cut pinions in the train, a lantern pinion to drive the dial motions, a seconds pendulum with anchor-recoil escapement, a contra cord for winding, triple-hung weights, and ratchets to drive the moon disc, calendar hand, and cam for annual motion of sunrise and sunset indicator.

condition
New corner blocks on back feet; spire of central finial missing.

provenance
Joe Kindig, Jr., York, Pa.; Francis P. Garvan, New York, N.Y.

bibliography
Antiques, 29 (March 1936), (illus. inside front cover); Dreppard, p. 168.

comments
An article in the *Maryland Gazette* of September, 1790, perhaps best describes this ingenious clock "completed by Mr. John Fischer, Sen., Yorktown, Pennsylvania, May 23, 1790; the astronomical part of which does the greatest honor to the inventor.

> This Timepiece performs the office of a common eight day clock, but runs thirty-five days; It exhibits the time of the Sun's rising and setting, its destination, the longest and shortest days in the most distant parts of the world, all of which is clearly elucidated by a globe, affixed about three inches from the centre; It has the moon circulating round the verge of the globe, which makes all the different vicissitudes that the real moon seems to make to us in the Heavens. The dial . . . plate is elegantly engraved, and is by no means void of taste; round the verge it is ornamented with the twelve signs of the Zodiac, the seven Planets, and twelve months, with the exact number of days in each month in a year.

(Prime, p. 249). Fisher was a brilliant mechanic who made a number of clocks that ran for more than one week. Astronomical clocks by American clockmakers are comparatively rare. A much more complex astronomical clock by David Rittenhouse is at the Drexel Institute, Philadelphia.

The Mabel Brady Garvan Collection
1936.307

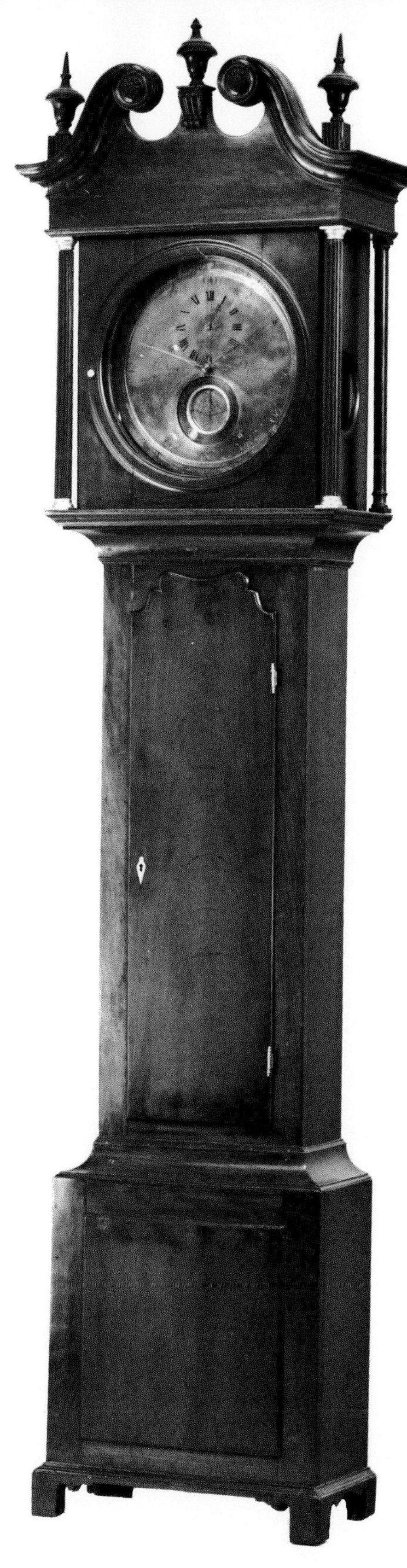

John Fisher
York Town
January
February
March
April
May
June
July
August
September
October
November
December

tall clocks
PENNSYLVANIA

Canonsburg, Pennsylvania, 1795–1800
"Will.m Wallace / Alex.r Cook / Canonsburgh No 14" engraved on dial.

woods
American black walnut; top of hood, cherry; backboard, white pine.

dimensions
CASE: MH. 97⅛ in. (246.8 cm); hood: W. 23 in. (58.9 cm), FW. 201/16 in. (51.0 cm), D. 11¾ in. (29.9 cm), FD. 10⅜ in. (26.4 cm); lower case: H. 61⅞ in. (157.2 cm), W. 17⅞ in. (45.4 cm), FW. 14 7/16 in. (37.0 cm), D. 9⅝ in. (24.5 cm), FD. 7⅞ in. (20.0 cm). *DIAL:* H. 18⅜ in. (46.7 cm), W. 13 in. (33.0 cm).
MOVEMENT: H. 6 9/16 in. (16.8 cm), W. 4 11/16 in. (12.0 cm), D. 2 9/16 in. (6.6 cm).

inscription
"Wilson" cast in intermediate plate between movement and dial facing main dial.

description
Hood with three bulb-shaped finials on fluted plinths, swan neck pediment with carved rosettes, fluted columns at the front corners, double serpentine boards at the rear corners, and a glazed door with an arched top. Waist with a cove molding at the top, fluted quarter columns at the front corners, and a door with a serpentine shaped top. Base with cove and ovolo moldings at the top, fluted quarter columns at the front corners, applied plaque with hollow upper corners, and ogee bracket feet.

Painted iron dial with roman hour numerals, arabic minute and second numerals, floral sprays in the spandrels, transfer-printed maps in front of the moon dial, seconds dial above the pierced hands and calendar dial and signature plate below.

Eight-day movement with brass plates and wheels, cut pinions, seconds pendulum, anchor-recoil escapement, smooth sheet-brass drums, two double-hung cast iron weights, and rack and snail striking system.

condition
Board facing dial replaced; crack in the frame of the glazed door repaired.

provenance
Paul N. and Olive L. Dann, New Haven, Conn.

comments
The American settlers who moved west after the Revolution brought with them their skills and trades. Canonsburgh, Pennsylvania, on Chartiers Creek, south of Pittsburgh, was laid out in 1787 by John Canon. Alexander Cook, a clockmaker whose name is engraved on the dial of this clock, was listed among the taxables when the borough of Canonsburgh was set up. The identity of William Wallace has not yet been established. The case of the clock is a fine example of rural Pennsylvania cabinetwork with its fluted quarter columns, carved rosettes on the swan neck pediment, and compass-rose decoration on the frieze. Other Alexander Cook clocks are also marked with an engraved brass plaque on a painted iron dial.

Bequest of Olive Louise Dann
1962.31.17

Willm. Wallace
Alexr. Cook
Canonſburgh

Probably Reading, Pennsylvania, 1801
"Benj.n Witman/ Reading" painted on dial.

woods
Birch; white pine.

dimensions
CASE: H. 95$\frac{9}{16}$ in. (242.7 cm); hood: W. 21¾ in. (52.7 cm), FW. 19¼ in. (48.9 cm), D. 11 in. (27.9 cm), FD. 9$\frac{9}{16}$ in. (24.3 cm); lower case: H. 62½ in. (158.7 cm), W. 19⅛ in. (48.6 cm), FW. 14 in. (35.6 cm), D. 9⅞ in. (25.1 cm), FD. 7¼ in. (18.4 cm).
DIAL: H. 17 in. (43.2 cm), W. 12 in. (30.5 cm).
MOVEMENT: H. 5¼ in. (13.3 cm), W. 4⅝ in. (11.8 cm), D. 2$\frac{5}{16}$ in. (5.9 cm).

inscription
Lower case door inlaid "CHR FAHL / 1801."

description
Hood with three urn-and-flame finials—the outer two on fluted plinths—a swan neck pediment with carved rosettes and dentilling, a tulip-and-leaf carved frieze with an arch at center front, freestanding turned columns at the four corners, arched sidelights, and a tulip-and-vine inlaid glazed door with an arched top. Waist with a cove molding at the top, an applied band of fretwork, floral carved quarter columns at the front corners, and an inlaid door with an arched top. Base with a cove molding at the top, paneled front, rope-and-rosette carved quarter columns at the front corners and ogee bracket feet.

Painted iron dial with roman hour numerals, arabic minute numerals, floral sprays in the spandrels and above the finely pierced hands, calendar aperture below the hands, and a painted eagle in the arched top.

Twenty-four hour movement with brass plates and wheels, cut pinions, the time train on the left, striking train on the right, seconds pendulum with anchor-recoil escapement, rack and snail repeating striking system, single weight-driven winding chain, and escape wheel turning counterclockwise (which accounts for the absence of a seconds dial).

condition
Finials replaced; rosettes and tops of scrolled pediment replaced; right rear foot restored; left rear foot repaired; left edge of waist door restored; shrinkage crack repaired in front panel of base; case refinished. Paint abraded on main and calendar dials; crudely replaced minute hand; pendulum hanger repaired; bell and bracket missing; lower dial feet reattached to dial.

provenance
Luke V. Lockwood, Greenwich, Conn.; Francis P. Garvan, New York, N.Y.

comments
This tall-clock case inlaid with the name "CHR FAHL" and the date 1801 is a superlative example of rural Pennsylvania craftsmanship and has many characteristic features of urban Philadelphia cabinetwork, such as quarter columns and a band of fretwork just below the hood. The profusion of fanciful ornament—the tulips and flowers carved on the pediment and quarter columns and also inlaid in wax and wood on the doors and base—reveals the clock's rural origin. The movement is signed by Benjamin Witman (1774–1857) of Reading, who may have been trained by his grandfather, Adam Witman, a clockmaker, innkeeper, and early settler of Reading (Albright, p. 47). The handsome, brightly colored dial may have been painted by Benjamin Witman, for in 1799 he advertised as a dial painter (Palmer, *Am. Clocks,* p. 307) and eventually seems to have given up clockmaking in favor of the dial-painting business.

The Mabel Brady Garvan Collection
1930.2281

CHR FAHL
1801

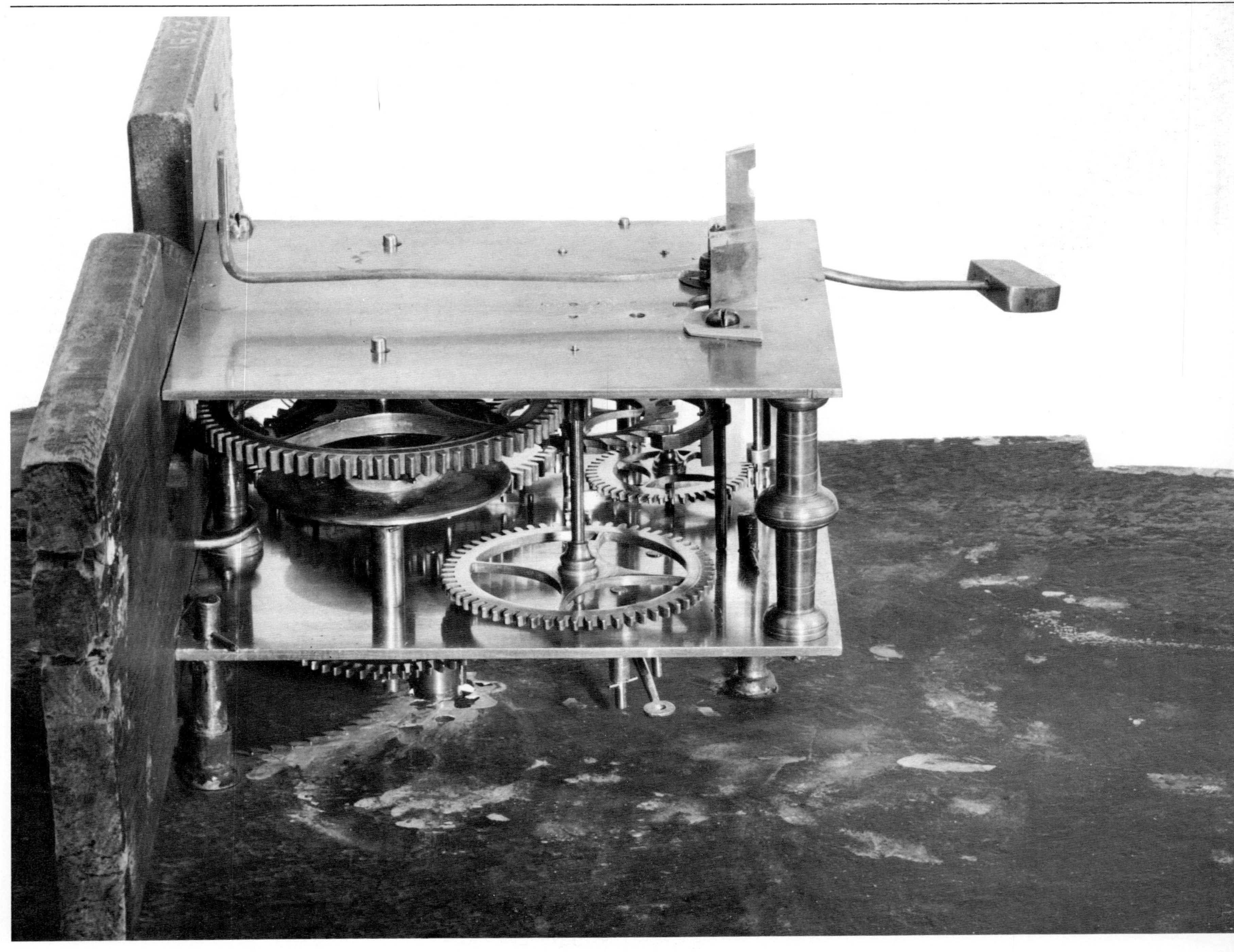

Benj. Witman
Reading

Probably Lancaster, Pennsylvania, 1810–1820
"John Hoff / LANCASTER" painted on dial.

woods
Cherry; white pine.

dimensions
CASE: H. 95¾ in. (243.2 cm); hood: W. 20⅛ in. (51.1 cm), FW. 18¾ in. (47.7 cm), D. 10$\frac{1}{16}$ in. (25.6 cm), FD. 9⅜ in. (23.9 cm); lower case: H. 67¼ in. (170.8 cm), W. 19 in. (48.3 cm), FW. 13$\frac{3}{16}$ in. (33.5 cm), D. 10$\frac{3}{16}$ in. (33.5 cm), FD. 7¼ in. (18.4 cm).
DIAL: H. 18½ in. (47.0 cm), W. 13 in. (33.0 cm).
MOVEMENT: H. 5¾ in. (14.6 cm), W. 5 in. (12.7 cm), D. 2⅜ in. (6.1 cm).

description
Hood with a spired urn finial, two inlaid plinths, a swan neck pediment with inlaid pinwheels, a frieze with an inlaid keystone and arch at center front, freestanding columns at the front corners, freestanding turned balusters at the rear corners, and a glazed door with an arched top. Waist with a cove molding at the top, a band of inlay in a pattern of circles, an inlaid eagle, chamfered and inlaid front corners, and a door with elliptical stringing and hollow upper corners. Base with a cove molded top, inlaid front corners, inlaid rectangle with hollow corners at the front, and a band of light and dark inlay above the French feet.

Painted iron dial with roman hour numerals and arabic minute numerals, painted fans in the spandrels, a seconds dial above the pierced hands and a calendar aperture below, and transfer-printed global maps flanking the moon dial.

Eight-day movement with brass plates and wheels, lantern pinions—the second pinion in each train open at one side—seconds pendulum with anchor-recoil escapement, smooth drums, two double-hung weights, and rack and snail striking system.

condition
Two finials missing; top of plinths new; three corner blocks replaced; back of left rear foot and side of right rear foot restored; case refinished; paint on dial abraded; hour hand replaced; movement rebushed; part of striking mechanism missing.

provenance
Joe Kindig, Jr., York, Pennsylvania; Francis P. Garvan, New York, N.Y.

bibliography
Theodore Sizer, "The Mabel Brady Garvan Collection of American Arts and Crafts," *Bulletin of the Association in Fine Arts at Yale University,* 4 (Dec. 1930), (illus. inside front cover); *Antiques,* May, 1929, p. 422.

comments
John Hoff was a particularly active clockmaker who worked in Lancaster, Pennsylvania, from 1800 to 1819. The Hoffs of Lancaster, along with Jacob Godschalk, his apprentice, Griffith Owen, and Jacob Hosteller, were among the few American clockmakers to make clocks with "lantern pinions" in the German tradition rather than the cut pinions preferred by French and English clockmakers (Montgomery, fig. 152). In the opinion of Edward LaFond, the Hoff family epitomizes the self-reliant tradition of inland Pennsylvania clockmakers. George, John's father, developed a system of manufacture using almost interchangeable parts so that the Hoffs did not have to rely on imported parts. At Winterthur a similar clock case—with an inlaid eagle, ropelike stringing outlining the front corners, and inlaid pinwheel terminals on the swan neck pediment—houses a movement by Jacob Eby of Manheim, Pennsylvania (Montgomery, fig. 153). Here the stripes in the eagle's shield are inlaid with red wax and the lines of his feathers are drawn, or "engraved," with black ink.

The Mabel Brady Garvan Collection
1930.2280

E PLURIBUS UNUM

John Hoff
LANCASTER

tall clocks

PENNSYLVANIA

Germantown, Pennsylvania, 1820–1840

"John Heilig Germantown" painted on dial.

woods

Mahogany; inner base molding on hood, cherry; top of hood, tulip; sides of case and hood, white pine.

dimensions

CASE: H. 98$^{15}/_{16}$ in. (251. 3 cm) ; hood: W. 21¾ in. (55.3 cm), FW. 20⅛ in. (51.1 cm), D. 11⅛ in. (28.3 cm), FD. 10¼ in. (26.1 cm) ; lower case: H. 66$^{1}/_{16}$ in. (167.8 cm), W. 22$^{5}/_{16}$ in. (56.7 cm), FW. 15⅞ in. (40.3 cm), D. 11¼ in. (28.6 cm), FD. 7⅞ in. (20.0 cm).
DIAL: H. 20 in. (50.8 cm), W. 14⅛ in. (35.9 cm).
MOVEMENT: H. 6 in. (15.3 cm), W. 4$^{15}/_{16}$ in. (12.6 cm), D. 2½ in. (6.3 cm).

description

Hood with three urn-and-pointed-bulb finials, swan neck pediment, frieze with a keystone and an arch at center front. Spiral-turned columns at the front corners, plain columns at the rear corners, and a glazed door with an arch at the top. Waist with a cove molding at the top, two turned columns at the front corners, and an applied panel below the door. Base with a cove and ovolo molding at the top, applied panel at the front, two thin bands of molding at the front and sides, and double ball turned feet.

Painted iron dial with roman hour numerals, arabic minute numerals, strawberries painted in the spandrels, a moon dial in the arch at the top flanked by transfer-printed global maps, a seconds dial above the center of the main dial, a day-of-the-month dial below, and pierced hour and minute hands.

Eight-day movement with brass plates and wheels, cut pinions, a seconds pendulum with anchor-recoil escapement, grooved drums, double-hung weights, and a rack and snail striking system.

condition

Both scrolls of pediment repaired.

exhibitions

Mrs. Nathalie Penrose Swetland, Hartford, Conn.

comments

John Heilig was a member of a large family of clockmakers who worked in Germantown, Pennsylvania. His grandfather Hendrick came from Hanover, Germany, and was the uncle of David and Benjamin Rittenhouse. John Heilig, who was born in 1765 and died in 1841, probably had a long career as a silversmith and clockmaker in Germantown. The dark figured mahogany veneer and double ball feet, reflecting the Empire style, suggest that this clock was probably made late in Heilig's career. The dial may possibly be American; the movement is nicely made.

Gift of Mrs. Nathalie Penrose Swetland in memory of William Rex Penrose
1966.87.18

John Heilig
Germantown

tall clocks

RHODE ISLAND

Providence, Rhode Island, 1753–1785

"Spalding. / Providence." engraved on dial.

woods

Soft maple; top of hood, tulip; back of hood, chestnut.

dimensions

CASE: 87⅜ in. (221.9 cm); hood: W. 20½ in. (52.1 cm), FW. 15½ in. (39.4 cm), D. 10¼ in. (26.1 cm), FD. 7½ in. (19.1 cm); lower case: H. 62⅝ in. (159.1 cm), W. 18⅝ in. (47.3 cm), FW. 13¾ in. (34.9 cm), D. 9⅛ in. (23.2 cm), FD. 6$\frac{9}{16}$ in. (16.7 cm).
DIAL: H. 17$\frac{1}{16}$ in. (43.4 cm), W. 12 in. (30.5 cm).
MOVEMENT: H. 6¾ in. (17.1 cm), W. 4$\frac{13}{16}$ in. (12.2 cm), D. 2½ in. (6.4 cm).

description

Hood with a cornice with an arch at center front, freestanding turned balusters at the four corners, and a glazed door with an arch at the top. Waist with a cove molding at the top and a door with an arched top. Base with ogee and ovolo moldings at the top, applied panel on the front, and straight bracket feet.

Cast brass dial with engraved roman hour numerals, arabic numerals and calendar dial on the brass chapter ring, cast brass rococo ornaments in the spandrels and flanking the "STRIKE/SILENT" dial in the arch at the top; stippled center, seconds dial above the pierced hour hand and signature plate below.

Eight-day movement with brass plates and wheels, cut pinions, seconds pendulum with anchor-recoil escapement, two double-hung weights, grooved winding drums, crank key for winding, and a rack and snail striking system.

condition

Cove molding applied to top of waist replaced; case refinished. Second hand replaced; minute and calendar hands missing; center wheel needs work; worn pivot holes disfigured by peening.

provenance

Francis P. Garvan, New York, N.Y.

comments

From his birthplace, the small eastern Connecticut town of Plainfield, Edward Spalding (1732–1785) probably went as a young man to Providence, Rhode Island, to be trained as a clockmaker. In his twenty-first year he engraved "Edward Spalding Providence 1753" on a clock which may have been his "masterpiece" (*Antiques,* Sept. 1940, fig. 7, p. 118). Two other Spalding clocks have long been owned by Rhode Island families (*Antiques,* Aug. 1942, p. 87). The maple case of the Yale clock is relatively simple compared to one of these, which has a handsome blocked and shell-carved mahogany case. The parts for the movement for the Yale clock were obviously imported from Europe, for the rococo style ornaments in the spandrels are identical to those on No. 18, by Moses Ogden of New Jersey. In the present clock the casting is not nearly as crisp.

The Mabel Brady Garvan Collection
1930.2325

STRIKE
SILENT

STRIKE
SILENT
Spalding
PROVIDENCE

35

Rhode Island, about 1785

woods
Mahogany; top of hood and a glueblock in case, basswood; back of hood, white pine.

dimensions
CASE: H. 88 in. (223.5 cm), MH. right finial, 89¼ in. (226.7 cm); hood: W. 22¼ in. (56.5 cm), FW. 16¹¹⁄₁₆ in. (42.4 cm), D. 11¼ in. (28.6 cm), FD. 8⅜ in. (21.3 cm); lower case: H. 61¼ in. (155.6 cm), W. 20³⁄₁₆ in. (51.3 cm), FW. 14¹¹⁄₁₆ in. (37.3 cm), D. 10³⁄₁₆ in. (25.9 cm), FD. 7⁷⁄₁₆ in. (18.9 cm).
DIAL: H. 18¾ in. (47.6 cm), W. 13⅛ in. (33.3 cm).
MOVEMENT: H. 6¹¹⁄₁₆ in. (17.0 cm), W. 4¹⁵⁄₁₆ in. (12.6 cm), D. 2¹¹⁄₁₆ in. (6.9 cm).

inscriptions
"Osborne's / Manufactory / Birmingham" cast in intermediate plate between movement and dial facing main dial; "Osborne's / Manufactory / Birmingham" stamped on moon and calendar dials.

description
Hood with two carved ball-and-acorn finials on fluted plinths, cornice with an arch at center front, freestanding fluted columns at the four corners, oval sidelights, and a glazed door with an arched top. Waist with a cove molding at the top and a blocked door with a rounded top and a carved shell at the top of the blocking. Base with an ogee molding at the top, applied panel at the front, and ogee bracket feet.

Painted iron dial with roman hour numerals, arabic minute numerals, painted floral sprays in the spandrels, transfer-printed global maps flanking the moon dial, a seconds dial above the pierced hands, and a calendar aperture below.

Eight-day movement with brass plates with trapezoidal openings at the bottom, brass wheels with distinctive collets, or hubs, cut pinions, smooth drums, two double-hung weights, and a rack and snail striking system.

condition
Finials replaced; parts of both rear feet and the left front foot restored; side of right front foot repaired; some corner blocks replaced; case refinished in 1963. Dial paint chipped over three of the four dial feet; calendar dial paint chipped; pivot holes worn.

provenance
Israel Sack, Inc., New York, N.Y.; Francis P. Garvan, New York, N.Y. (1929).

bibliography
Albert Sack, *Fine Points of Furniture: Early American* (New York: Crown Publishers, 1950), p. 122 (illus. lower left corner).

comments
The movement of this clock is unsigned, but the blocked, shell-carved door of the case immediately suggests Rhode Island cabinetwork. The movement of a similar tall clock was signed by Seril Dodge of Providence in 1784 or 1785. Both clocks are decorated with delicate ogee feet, applied panels on the base, and freestanding fluted columns on the hood (Joseph K. Ott, *The John Brown House Loan Exhibition of Rhode Island Furniture* [Rhode Island Historical Society, 1965], p. 78). "Osborne's / Manufactory / Birmingham" cast in the intermediate plate between the dial and movement indicates that the dials, at least, were imported from England. The numerals for the days of the month are particularly small. The unusual design of the pear-shaped collets holding the gears to the shafts may be a clue to the maker of this movement.

The Mabel Brady Garvan Collection
1930.2286

tall clocks
SOUTH CAROLINA

Charleston, South Carolina, about 1795
"PAT,^{k} MAGANN/ Charleston" painted on dial.

woods
Mahogany; white pine.

dimensions
CASE: H. 98¾ in. (250.8 cm); hood: W. 20¾ in. (52.7 cm), FW. 18⅝ in. (47.3 cm), D. 10⅜ in. (26.4 cm), FD. 9⅜ in. (23.8 cm); lower case: H. 64⅜ in. (163.5 cm), W. 19 in. (48.3 cm), FW. 14⅛ in. (35.9 cm), D. 9½ in. (24.1 cm), FD. 6 15/16 in. (17.6 cm).
DIAL: H. 18⅜ in. (46.7 cm), W. 13⅛ in. (33.3 cm).
MOVEMENT: H. 6⅝ in. (16.8 cm), W. 4½ in. (11.4 cm), D. 2½ in. (6.4 cm).

inscription
"ASHWIN & CO." cast in skeleton plate between dial and movement.

description
Hood with an urn and brass eagle finial, broken arch pediment, frieze with an applied brass band, freestanding multiple ring-turned columns at the front corners, quarter columns at the rear corners, and a glazed door with an arched top. Waist with a cove molding at the top and a door with a rounded top. Base with an ogee molding at the top and a baseboard with ogee arches on the front and sides.

Painted iron dial with roman hour numerals, arabic minute numerals, gilded arabesques in the spandrels, seconds dial above the pierced hands and a calendar aperture below, transfer-printed global maps flanking the moon dial in the arch at the top.

Eight-day movement with brass plates and wheels, cut pinions, seconds pendulum with anchor-recoil escapement, smooth drums, two double-hung weights, and a rack and snail striking system.

condition
Case refinished; eagle finial new, paint worn and chipped on dial; some minute numerals repainted; all hands replaced; one dial foot repaired; the feet on the false plate now attached to movement by modern screws; main wheel in strike train has a patch soldered on one side, another wheel in poor condition; center post was bent.

provenance
Francis P. Garvan, New York, N.Y.

comments
The first mention of Patrick Magann in America appeared in the *Charleston City Gazette and Advertiser* on February 29, 1792, when he advertised as a "Watch and Clock-Maker, lately from Ireland, who wrought in said branches in the first places of that kingdom, particularly Dublin and Belfast." He advertised again in 1794 to announce a new business location and the need for an apprentice, probably an indication that his business was prosperous. The case may have been made in South Carolina, although the similarity of the turnings on the columns on the hood to columns on two Massachusetts pieces at Yale, a card table (1930.2700) and a stand (1930.2659), raise the possibility that the case was imported from the north.

The Mabel Brady Garvan Collection
1930.2021

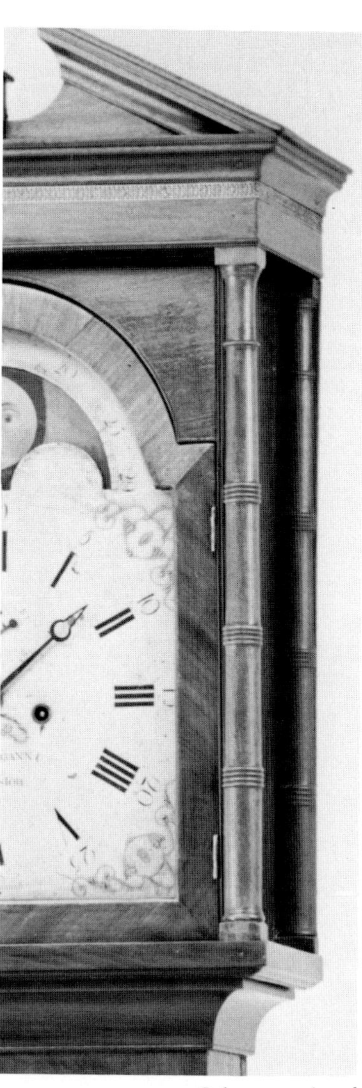

Column on hood

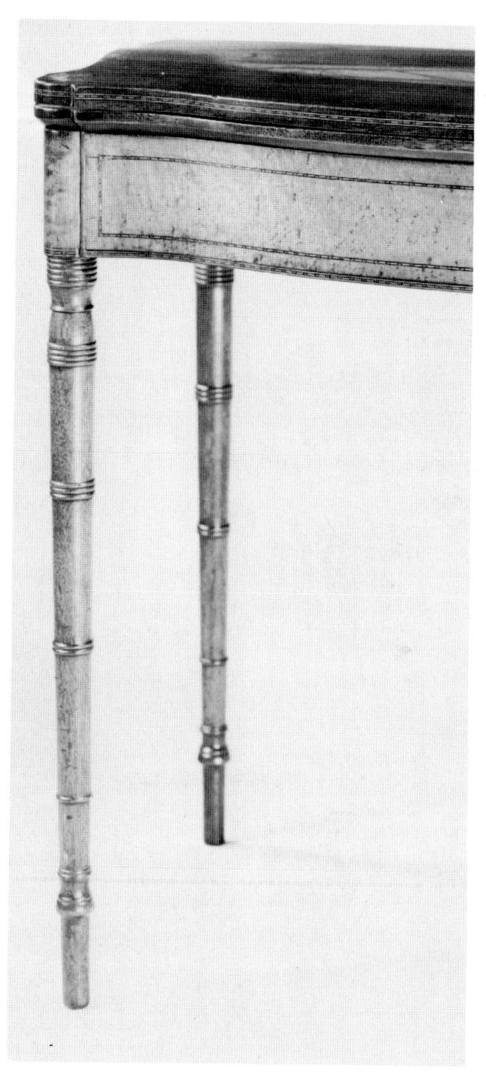

Leg of card table
(Garvan Collection 1930.2700)

PAT^K MAGANN
Charleston

shelf clocks

Newburyport, Massachusetts, about 1800
"David Wood,/ Newburyport" painted on dial.

woods
Mahogany; backboard and glueblocks, white pine.

dimensions
CASE: H. 37½ in. (95.2 cm); hood: W. 11½ in. (29.3 cm), FW. 10 in. (25.4 cm), D. 6 in. (15.2 cm), FD. 5¼ in. (13.4 cm); lower case: H. 16¾ in. (42.5 cm), W. 11½ in. (29.2 cm), FW. 9 15/16 in. (25.2 cm), D. 6 in. (15.2 cm), FD. 5 3/16 in. (13.2 cm).
DIAL: H. 9¾ in. (24.8 cm), W. 7 in. (17.8 cm).
MOVEMENT: H. 4½ in. (11.4 cm), W. 2 13/16 in. (7.2 cm), D. 1½ in. (3.8 cm).

description
Hood with three brass ball and eagle finials on fluted plinths connected by an arched crest, arched and cove molded cornice, arched sidelights, a glazed door with an arched top, and a cove molding at the base. Base with an astragal molding at the top, fluted quarter columns at the front corners, oval escutcheons and bail handles on the sides, veneered door, a band of scalloped inlay on the front and sides, serpentine curved skirts, and French feet.

Painted iron dial with roman hour numerals, arabic minute numerals, painted diaper pattern in the spandrels, gilt paterae and arabesques in the arched top, and pierced hands.

Eight-day movement with brass plates and wheels, cut pinions in the time train, anchor-recoil escapement, an eighteen-inch pendulum and smooth winding drums one and one-eighth inches in diameter.

condition
Brass capital on left column replaced; brass finials cracked and corroded; cornice molding on right side restored; right side of arched pediment replaced; refinished.

provenance
Charles W. Lyon, New York, N.Y.; Francis P. Garvan, New York, N.Y.

comments
Of the Massachusetts shelf clocks in the Winterthur collection Charles Montgomery writes: "Without counterpart in the Middle-Atlantic or Southern regions, Massachusetts shelf clocks—usually with eight-day movements similar to those used in 'banjo' timepieces—were being made by most of the important New England clockmakers by 1800. Designed for a less affluent market than the purchasers of tall clocks, the shelf clocks required but one-third the quantity of brass needed for tall clocks; and, although some cases, notably those for David Wood and Willard movements, were elegant indeed, many were but simple pine boxes. Their popularity waned by 1830 when the market was filled by inexpensive machine-made shelf clocks." (Montgomery, p. 193.) The highly figured veneer on the door of this shelf clock by David Wood immediately focuses attention on a case which is treated with a number of other fine details, such as the simple lunette-patterned inlaid band on the base, the inlaid quarter columns, bail handles on the sides, and the delicate hands with heart-shaped motifs. David Wood, who worked in Newburyport from about 1792 to 1824, is best known for his shelf clocks, although one of his tall clocks is represented in this collection (No. 15).

The Mabel Brady Garvan Collection
1930.2096

David Wood
Newburyport

shelf clocks

MASSACHUSETTS

Concord, Massachusetts, 1800–1810

"Nath[l] Munroe / CONCORD " painted on dial.

woods

Mahogany; glueblocks, white pine.

dimensions

CASE: H. 39¼ in. (99.7 cm); hood: W. 11⅜ in. (28.9 cm), FW. 10¼ in. (26.1 cm), D. 5 in. (12.7 cm), FD. 4⅜ in. (11.2 cm); lower case: H. 16 3/16 in. (41.1 cm), W. 11⅜ in. (28.9 cm), FW. 10 3/16 in. (25.9 cm), D. 5 in. (12.7 cm), FD. 4⅜ in. (11.1 cm).
DIAL: H. 11¼ in. (28.6 cm), W. 8 in. (20.3 cm).
MOVEMENT: H. 4¼ in. (10.8 cm), W. 2⅛ in. (5.4 cm), D. 1⅝ in. (4.2 cm).

description

Hood with three brass urn-shaped finials—the center one on an inlaid plinth flanked by fretwork—a pagoda-shaped pediment, veneered and inlaid door with a bell-shaped glass, and a cove molding at the bottom. Base with veneer and stringing at the front, serpentine curved skirts, and French feet.

Painted bell-shaped iron dial with roman hour numerals, signature in a gilt oval, and long dart-shaped hour and minute hands.

Eight-day movement with brass plates and wheels, cut pinions, anchor-recoil escapement, 10½-inch pendulum, double-hung weights on the time train, and a bell marked "G. Ainsworth Warr."

condition

Horizontal shrinkage cracks on front of base; front of right foot replaced; refinished.

provenance

Paul N. and Olive L. Dann, New Haven, Conn.

comments

The "Concord" painted on the dial of this clock refers to the Massachusetts town, not to be confused with Concord, New Hampshire. Nathaniel Munroe (1777–1861), who worked with his brother Daniel between 1800 and 1807, ran a large business that specialized in the making of brass movements. With its cove- and ovolo-molded top and bell-shaped glass, this shelf clock is strikingly different from the preceding example. Here the serpentine curves of the skirts and the French feet are not handled as surely and give the clock a less elegant appearance.

Bequest of Olive L. Dann
1962.31.27

Movement seen from above

Nathl. Munroe
CONCORD

shelf clocks

MASSACHUSETTS

Boston, Massachusetts, 1800–1810

"Aaron Willard / BOSTON" painted on dial.

woods

Mahogany; backboard, white pine.

dimensions

CASE: H. 39½ in. (100.3 cm); hood: H. 10 15/16 in. (27.8 cm), FW. 9½ in. (24.8 cm), D. 5⅝ in. (14.3 cm), FD. 5¼ in. (13.4 cm); lower case: H. 16⅞ in. (42.9 cm), W. 10⅞ in. (27.6 cm), FW. 9¾ in. (24.8 cm), D. 5⅝ in. (14.3 cm), FD. 5 5/16 in. (13.5 cm).

DIAL: H. 11¼ in. (28.6 cm), W. 8 3/16 in. (20.8 cm).

MOVEMENT: H. 4⅝ in. (11.8 cm), W. 2 15/16 in. (7.5 cm), D. 1 11/16 in. (4.3 cm).

description

The case of this clock is very similar to the preceding example, No. 38. Here there is only one finial on the hood and the square cornice and frame on either side of the door are decorated with stringing. The patterns of the veneer and inlay on the base are likewise somewhat different.

Painted bell-shaped iron dial with roman hour numerals, gilt leaves and pendant drops around the signature near the bottom, and pointed hour and minute hands.

Eight-day movement with brass plates and wheels, cut pinions, anchor-recoil escapement, 14½-inch pendulum, smooth winding drum, and a double-hung weight on the time train.

condition

Fretwork repaired on left side and restored on right side; pediment repaired; refinished.

provenance

Fred Wellington Ayer, Bangor, Me. (sale New York, American Art Galleries, American Art Association, Inc., May 3–4, 1929); Francis P. Garvan, New York, N.Y.

comments

Bell- or kidney-shaped dials and what are known as "bell-top" cases appear in America on Massachusetts shelf clocks made in the early part of the nineteenth century, such as the example illustrated. Such decorative ideas come at the end of a long tradition of ornamentation of English bracket clocks. The "bell-top" cases of English clocks were introduced in the last years of the seventeenth century and can be found as late as 1780 on a bracket clock by John Elliott (Britten, fig. 798). A bell-shaped dial whose lower edge is serpentine can be found on an English table clock made by George Graham about 1735–40, the whole form of which follows the outline of the dial (Percy Macquoid and Ralph Edwards, *Dictionary of English Furniture* [London, 1924] II, 116). The double case form of the Massachusetts shelf clock is peculiar to America and is unlike the small compact shape of the English bracket clock. The American clocks relied on weights for motive power, whereas the small English clocks usually have spring-powered movements. The hands of this clock are typical of Aaron Willard's work, as is the very thin escape wheel.

The Mabel Brady Garvan Collection
1930.2341

Aaron Willard
BOSTON

40

Boston, Massachusetts, 1800–1810
"Aaron Willard,/ BOSTON" painted on dial.

woods
Mahogany; backboard, white pine.

dimensions
CASE: H. 31¾ in. (80.6 cm); hood: W. 11³⁄₁₆ in. (28.4 cm), FW. 10½ in. (26.7 cm), D. 4⅞ in. (12.4 cm), FD. 4⅜ in. (11.1 cm); lower case: H. 13¾ in. (34.9 cm), W. 11³⁄₁₆ in. (28.4 cm), FW. 10½ in. (26.7 cm), D. 4⅞ in. (12.4 cm), FD. 4⅜ in. (11.1 cm).
DIAL: H. 11 in. (27.9 cm), W. 8⅛ in. (20.6 cm).
MOVEMENT: H. 4⁷⁄₁₆ in. (11.3 cm), W. 2¾ in. (7.0 cm), D. 1⁹⁄₁₆ in. (4.0 cm).

description
Hood with a central plinth, pierced fretwork, square cornice with stringing, door with a bell-shaped glass and a cove molding at the bottom. Base with veneer, stringing, and crossbanding on the front, ogee-molded baseboard and ogee bracket feet.

Painted bell-shaped iron dial with roman hour numerals, arabic minute numerals, bowknots, floral swags and gilt arabesques around the signature near the base, and dart-shaped hour and minute hands.

Eight-day movement with brass plates and wheels, cut pinions, anchor-recoil escapement, 10½-inch pendulum and double-hung weights.

condition
Ogee bracket feet and blocks replaced; fretwork replaced; finial missing; molding on top of left side repaired; refinished.

provenance
Charles B. Stetson, Boston, Mass.

comments
The ogee bracket feet on this clock case are new, but the two-stage base molding suggests that they replace similar originals. This feature is stylistically earlier than the French feet on the preceding Willard clock, No. 39. The gilt arabesques and floral swags surrounding the signature are quite elaborate. The replaced fretwork is not very convincingly done.

Bequest of Charles B. Stetson
1954.37.22

Aaron Willard,
BOSTON.

shelf clocks

MASSACHUSETTS

41

Boston, Massachusetts, 1815–1820
"Aaron Willard / BOSTON" painted on upper glass panel.

woods
Mahogany; backboard, white pine; blocks below movement, cherry.

dimensions
CASE: H. 34⅜ in. (87.3 cm); hood, W. 11⅝ in. (29.6 cm), FW. 10½ in. (26.7 cm), D. 5¹⁄₁₆ in. (12.9 cm), FD. 4⁹⁄₁₆ in. (11.7 cm); lower case: H. 13¹¹⁄₁₆ in. (34.8 cm), W. 11⅝ in. (29.5 cm), FW. 10⁷⁄₁₆ in. (26.5 cm), D. 5 in. (12.7 cm), FD. 4⅝ in. (11.7 cm).
DIAL: Diam. 8 in. (20.3 cm).
MOVEMENT: H. 4⅛ in. (10.5 cm), W. 2¼ in. (5.7 cm), D. 1⅝ in. (4.2 cm).

inscription
"208" stamped inside door on lower edge of frame, inside lower panel on edge of frame, and on backboard.

description
Hood with a flattened ball and spired brass finial on a reeded plinth, scrolled veneered pediment, half-round molded cornice, door with rounded molding and painted glass, and a cove and ovolo molding at the bottom. Base with rounded molding and painted glass at the front, ovolo-molded base and brass flattened ball feet.

Concave painted iron dial with roman hour numerals and pointed hour and minute hands.

Eight-day movement with brass plates and wheels, cut pinions, anchor-recoil escapement, a twelve-inch pendulum, and double hung weights on the hour train.

condition
Lower glass panel replaced in 1917; feet and finial replaced; refinished in 1963.

provenance
Charles Stetson, Boston, Mass.

comments
A similar shelf clock purchased by Louisa Adams in 1817, the year of her marriage (Randall, fig. 211), suggests that this clock and the following, No. 42, were made about the same time. The number "208" stamped on the backboard and the frames of both glass panels on this clock and the number "231" stamped on No. 42 may indicate that they were part of a numbered series. The lower glass panel on the present clock dates from 1917; it may replace a similar original or a mirror, like the one on the following example. The concave shape of this dial is quite different from those on any of the preceding examples.

Bequest of Charles B. Stetson
1954.37.23

Boston, Massachusetts, 1815–1820

"Aaron Willard / BOSTON" painted on upper glass panel.

woods
Mahogany; backboard, white pine; block below movement, birch.

dimensions
CASE: H. 35½ in. (90.2 cm); hood: W. 11 5/16 in. (28.9 cm), FW. 10½ in. (26.7 cm), D. 4 15/16 in. (12.6 cm), FD. 4 11/16 in. (12.0 cm); lower case: 13½ in. (34.3 cm), W. 11 5/16 in. (28.7 cm), FW. 10 7/16 in. (26.5 cm), D. 4 15/16 in. (12.5 cm), FD. 4½ in. (11.4 cm).
DIAL: Diam. 8 in. (20.3 cm).
MOVEMENT: H. 3⅞ in. (9.9 cm), W. 2⅝ in. (6.8 cm), D. 1 9/16 in. (4.0 cm).

inscription
"231" stamped inside door on lower edge.

description
See No. 41. The front of the base is a mirror rather than painted glass, and the brass feet are the bases of columns of the kind used on tall clock cases.

condition
Pediment and finial replaced; paint on the glass panel slightly damaged; refinished. The blocks attached to the seat board on either side of the movement are not original.

provenance
Paul N. and Olive L. Dann, New Haven, Conn.

comments
The replaced pediment, which lacks the highly figured veneer found on No. 41, and the absence of a glass panel in the base make this shelf clock less successful than the preceding example.

Bequest of Olive L. Dann
1962.31.18

shelf clocks
CONNECTICUT

43

Plymouth, Connecticut, about 1816
"Eli Terry, Plymouth, Con" printed on paper label.

woods
Mahogany; backboard, tulip; base, cherry; secondary wood in case, white oak.

dimensions
CASE: H. 28⅞ in. (73.3 cm), W. 16⅞ in. (42.9 cm), D. 4⅛ in. (10.5 cm).
DIAL: H. 11¼ in. (28.6 cm), W. 13 in. (33.0 cm).
MOVEMENT: H. 6¼ in. (15.9 cm), W. 7½ in. (19.0 cm), D. 1⅞ in. (4.6 cm).

inscriptions
"PATENT. / INVENTED, / Made and Sold by / Eli Terry, / Plymouth, / Con / N. B. To wind up the weights, put on the crank with the . . . . and turn towards Figure 6." Variation of the Sun and Clock also included on paper label on inside of backboard.

description
Case with three brass urn finials on plinths, scrolled veneered pediment, turned columns at the front corners, wooden strips at the back corners, door with clear glass above and painted glass below, cove and ovolo base moldings, serpentine curved skirts, and French feet.

Painted wooden dial with arabic hour and minute numerals, painted flowers and gilt decoration in the spandrels, anchor-recoil escapement above the center of the dial, and pierced pewter hands.

Twenty-four-hour movement with oak plates, cherry wheels and laurel pinions, separate double-hung weights for the time and strike trains, a count wheel partly recessed into the front plate to control the strike hammer, a pendulum between the dial and hands, and a bell attached to the dial below the movement.

condition
Both front and right rear legs repaired; upper glass cracked; paint on the glass panel damaged; scrolls of pediment repaired; finials new; refinished.

provenance
Paul N. and Olive L. Dann, New Haven, Conn.

comments
Shortly after completing his apprenticeship with Daniel Burnap in East Windsor, Connecticut, Eli Terry moved his business to Plymouth, Connecticut, in 1793. There he made tall clocks of both brass and wood. At first he produced them in small numbers, but during the first decade of the nineteenth century he gradually improved his methods of manufacture and increased production markedly. Terry sold his very successful business in 1810, and following a brief hiatus, he introduced a revolutionary idea to the clockmaking industry—the shelf clock with wooden movement of the type illustrated here, which he patented in 1816. The shelf clock had a number of distinct advantages over the tall clock. The escapement was placed outside the movement where it was easily accessible for maintenance. The gearing for the hands which needed little attention was placed inside the movement. The winding cords were brought up to the top of the case and were put over pulleys so that the full height of the case was utilized for the drop of the weights. These small clocks whose manufacture was adapted to techniques of mass-production opened a lucrative new era in the clock industry. The clocks take their name "pillar and scroll" from the nicely made mahogany cases with thin colonnettes flanking the doors and the scrolled, swan neck pediments.

Bequest of Olive L. Dann
1962.31.26

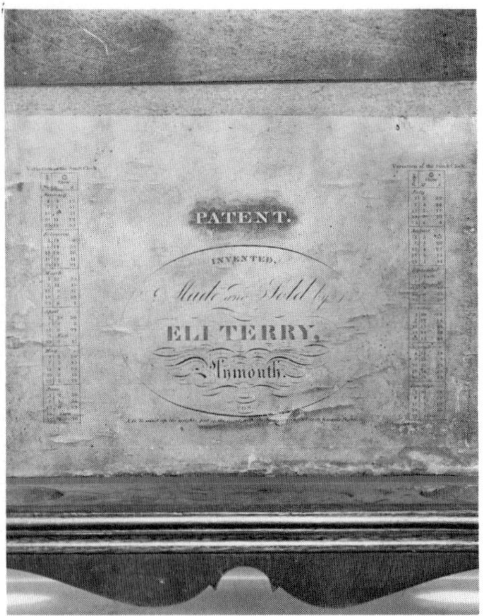

Movement seen from below

Movement seen from above

12
1
2
3
4
5
6
7
8
9
10
11
60
15
30
45

44

Bristol, Connecticut, 1839–1840

"JEROMES, GILBERT, GRANT & CO. / BRISTOL, CONN." printed on paper label.

woods
Mahogany, mahogany veneer, white pine.

dimensions
CASE: H. 25$^{15}/_{16}$ in. (65.8 cm), W. 15$^{7}/_{16}$ in. (39.2 cm), D. 4$^{7}/_{16}$ in. (11.3 cm).
DIAL: Diam. 7$^{11}/_{16}$ in. (9.5 cm).
MOVEMENT: H. 4¾ in. (12.1 cm), W. 5⅞ in. (15.1 cm), D. 2¾ in. (7.0 cm).

inscription
"PATENT/ BRASS CLOCKS,/ MADE AND SOLD BY/ JEROMES, GILBERT, GRANT & CO./ BRISTOL, CONN./ WARRANTED GOOD./ DIRECTIONS FOR SETTING THE CLOCK RUNNING AND KEEPING IT IN ORDER./ N.B. The clock can be set running without taking off the hands or dial plate. Put the pendulum through/ the loop at the end of the wire at the bottom of the dial, and hang it in the stud above./ Oil the pallets on ends of the part commonly called the verge, the pin on which the verge plays,/ and the wire/ which carries the pendulum at the place where it touches the rod. One drop of oil is sufficient for the whole./ Care should be taken not to wind the clock until the cord is put upon the pulley in the partition, and also on the/ top of the case, and the weights put on. The light weight on the strike side of the Clock./ To wind up the weights put on the key with the handle down, turn towards the figure six, and turn steadily until/ the weight is up./ If the hands want moving, do it by means of the longest, turning it at any time forward, but never backward/ when the Clock is within fifteen minutes of striking; and in no case no farther than to carry the minute hand up to/ figure XII./ DIRECTIONS FOR REGULATING THE CLOCK./ This is done by means of a screw at the bottom of the pendulum. If the Clock should go too fast, Lower the ball,/ if too slow raise it./ Printed by Elihu Geer, 26½ State-street, Hartford, Conn."

description
A shelf clock with an ogee-molded case surrounded by flat molding, a glazed door with black and gold painted decoration in the upper section and a transfer-printed scene, "Public Square New Haven." in the lower section.

Round stamped brass dial with roman hour numerals, heavy and thin black lines marking the minutes in the perimeter encompassing the hour numerals, and an opening at the center for the hour and minute hands.

Thirty-hour movement with wrought brass skeletonized plates, wrought brass wheels with cut teeth, lantern pinions, anchor-recoil escapement outside the front plate, twelve-hour count wheel mounted concentric with the second arbor and driven by a one-tooth pinion, and two double-hung weights.

condition
Glass in the lower section replaced.

provenance
Yale University.

comments
The gentlemen who formed "Jeromes, Gilbert, Grant & Co." were Chauncey and Noble Jerome, William L. Gilbert, and Zelotes Grant, partners for a brief period (1839–40) in Bristol, Connecticut. Chauncey Jerome, the most renowned, whose experiences in the clockmaking industry are recorded in his autobiographical *History of the American Clock Business*, introduced his famous O.G. clocks with thirty-hour brass movements at this time. Jerome had begun his career as a joiner making cases for Eli Terry's pillar and scroll clocks. By 1821 he had his own business in Bristol, and he continued to manufacture wooden clocks in the 1830's.

Wooden movements had dominated the Connecticut clock industry, but the emphasis was soon to change to brass. Wooden clocks had a number of disadvantages. They took longer to manufacture and were affected by moisture so that they could not be shipped long distances by water. In 1830 Joseph Ives, another Bristol clockmaker, returned from Brooklyn where he had developed a shelf clock with brass works, which he began to produce. An important factor contributing to the feasibility of manufacturing brass clocks was the establishment of the rolled brass industry in Waterbury, Connecticut. Fabrication of brass in this manner began between 1806 and 1808, and by 1830 the firm of Holmes and Hotchkiss started supplying the open market with sheet and wire (Roberts, p. 29).

The depression of 1837 badly hurt the Connecticut clock industry, and it was then that Chauncey Jerome conceived his less expensive thirty-hour brass clock. Increased mechanization in the production of this clock—punching out the wheels from thinner rolled brass and making the O.G. cases from wood shaped by running it through a power-operated machine—contributed to the reduced cost (Roberts, p. 33). Because the movements were brass, not wood, the clocks could be shipped long distances by water, enabling Jerome to capture new markets in the West, the South, and in England. Jerome's adaptation of new methods of technology to the manufacture of the brass thirty-hour clocks marks them as important products of the American Industrial Revolution.

PUBLIC SQUARE NEW HAVEN.

PATENT
BRASS CLOCKS,
MADE AND SOLD BY
JEROMES, GILBERT, GRANT & CO.
BRISTOL, CONN.
WARRANTED GOOD.
DIRECTIONS FOR SETTING THE CLOCK RUNNING AND KEEPING IT IN ORDER.

wall clocks

wall clocks

MASSACHUSETTS

45

Salem, Massachusetts, 1805–1809

"JABEZ BALDWIN. / SALEM." painted on lower glass panel.

woods
Mahogany; console, white pine.

dimensions
CASE: H. 45¼ in. (114.9 cm), W. 11⅝ in. (29.5 cm), D. 3¾ in. (9.5 cm).
DIAL: Diam. 7⅞ in. (20.0 cm).
MOVEMENT: H. 4⅜ in. (11.1 cm), W. 2¾ in. (7.0 cm), D. 1⅝ in. (4.2 cm).

inscriptions
Written in pink paint on back of lower glass panel: "Willard and Nolen— Boston / 5"

description
A wall clock with a gilt eagle finial on a plinth, circular convex glass door with brass bezel and latch, pierced brass side brackets, pink and gold glass panels in crossbanded and inlaid frames—the lower panel with an eagle, pendulum peephole, and signature—and gilt bracket with an acorn drop.

Round painted iron dial with roman hour numerals and spear-shaped hour and minute hands.

Eight-day movement with brass plates and wheels, cut pinions, double-hung lead weights, anchor-recoil escapement with small escape wheel, pendulum suspended below center post and a 3¼-inch pendulum bob.

condition
Wings of eagle finial repaired; case refinished; center post broken at hand pin hole.

provenance
Henry V. Weil, New York, N.Y.; Francis P. Garvan, New York, N.Y.

comments
A very similar clock at Winterthur bears the inscription "S. Willard's Patent" and is thought to have been made at his "Clock Manufactory" in Roxbury (Montgomery, fig. 159). The Yale clock is inscribed "Jabez Baldwin, Salem." The glass panels on both clocks are signed "Willard and Nolen." A narrow date range is given to this clock since Aaron Willard, Jr., and his brother-in-law Spencer Nolen were ornamental painters in partnership in Boston only from 1805 to 1809. According to Edward LaFond, the movement of this clock with the upside-down verge escapement coming off the bottom of the movement is almost identical to a "diamond head banjo" by Jabez Baldwin at Winterthur (Montgomery, fig. 161). Here, the three o'clock position of the winding hole is different.

The Mabel Brady Garvan Collection
1930.2194

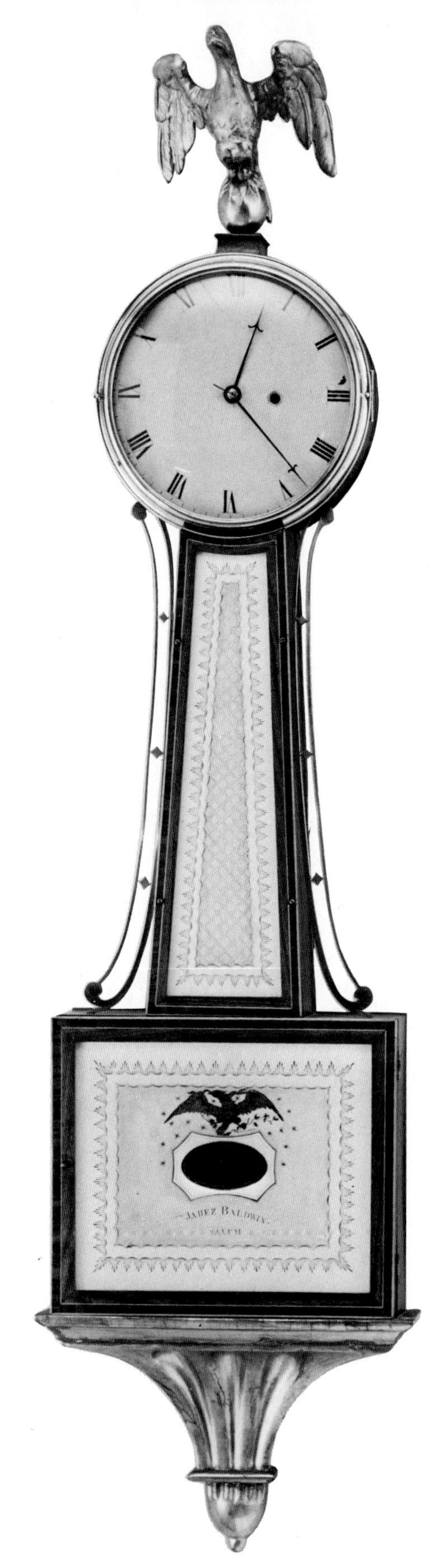
JABEZ BALDWIN

46

Massachusetts, 1802–1810

"WILLARD'S PATENT" painted below shield on lower glass panel.

woods
Mahogany; backboard, birch; glueblock, spruce (replaced?).

dimensions
CASE: H. 34¼ in. (87.0 cm), W. 10 in. (25.4 cm), D. 3⅜ in. (8.6 cm).
DIAL: Diam 7¾ in. (20.0 cm).
MOVEMENT: H. 4¼ in. (10.8 cm), W. 2⅝ in. (6.7 cm), D. 1$\frac{9}{16}$ in. (4.0 cm).

description
A wall clock with a brass spired ball finial on plinth, circular convex glass door with brass bezel and latch, pierced brass side brackets, and gold, white, and pinkish-gray glass panels in veneered and inlaid frames—the lower one with a scene of two female figures representing Liberty and Justice flanking a shield below the eagle.

Round painted iron dial with arabic hour numerals and spear-shaped hour and minute hands.

Eight-day movement with brass plates and wheels, cut pinions, double-hung weight, stepped train, curved crutch wire, 23¾ inch pendulum with a 3⅛ inch bob suspended from a T-bridge.

condition
Minor repair to crossbanding; new glue blocks in base; brass side brackets restored; case refinished.

Movement rebushed; bridge applied over minute wheel and idler in dial train in order to repair idler stud broken at pin hole.

provenance
Francis P. Garvan, New York, N.Y.

comments
The arabic numerals on the dial and more florid decoration on the glass panels gives this clock a less restrained appearance than that of No. 45. The patriotic scene on the lower door in which Liberty and Justice are symbolized is signed "Willard's Patent." This does not necessarily indicate that the clock was made in Willard's shop, for he permitted other people to sign their clocks in this way.

The Mabel Brady Garvan Collection
1930.2168

wall clocks
MASSACHUSETTS

Roxbury, Massachusetts, 1802–1810
"Warranted by Wm Cummens / ROXBURY" painted on dial.

woods
Mahogany; backboard, white pine.

dimensions
CASE: H. 34 11/16 in. (88.1 cm), W. 10 in. (25.4 cm), D. 4 in. (10.2 cm).
DIAL: Diam. 7¾ in. (20.0 cm).
MOVEMENT: H. 4 in. (10.2 cm), W. 2 11/16 in. (6.8 cm), D. 1½ in. (3.8 cm).

description
A wall clock with a wooden spired urn finial on an ovolo-molded plinth, circular convex glass door with a brass bezel and latch, pierced brass brackets, white, red, blue, green, and gold glass panels in gilded frames—the lower one painted with a village scene.

Round painted iron dial with roman hour numerals and spear-shaped hour and minute hands.

Eight-day movement with brass plates and wheels, cut pinions, anchor-recoil escapement, and a double-hung weight.

condition
Finial replaced; white paint on glass panel slightly damaged; wood refinished; paint chipped on dial; movement rebushed.

provenance
Mrs. Francis Wolfe Carey, Haddonfield, N.J.; Francis P. Garvan, New York, N.Y. (1928).

comments
William Cummens was an apprentice of Simon Willard's and had a long career as a clockmaker in Roxbury, from about 1789 to 1834. The very colorful glass tablets on this clock are probably the work of the painter Charles Bullard.

The Mabel Brady Garvan Collection
1930.2348

ROXBURY

wall clocks

MASSACHUSETTS

48

Boston, Massachusetts, about 1825.
"A. Willard J^r^" painted on dial.

woods
Mahogany; glueblocks, white pine.

dimensions
CASE: H. 39½ in. (100.3 cm), W. 9¹³⁄₁₆ in. (24.9 cm), D. 4³⁄₁₆ in. (10.6 cm).
DIAL: Diam. 7½ in. (19.1 cm).
MOVEMENT: H. 4½ in. (11.4 cm), W. 3 in. (7.6 cm), D. 1½ in. (3.8 cm).

description
A wall clock with a brass eagle finial on a domed plinth, circular convex glass door with a brass bezel and latch, pierced brass brackets, red, blue, gold, and white glass panels—the lower one labelled "AURORA"—in gilded frames with composition twist ornament, and a gilt bracket with composition balls and acorn drop.

Round painted iron dial with roman hour numerals and spear-shaped hour and minute hands.

Eight-day movement with brass plates with arches at the bottom to accommodate the bell, a rack and snail strike, two double-hung weights, stepped train, smooth winding drums, anchor-recoil escapement, 23½ inch pendulum with keystone opening around center post, and a 2¾ inch pendulum bob.

condition
Top of plinth replaced; rope ornament at top of waist missing, mahogany refinished; bracket probably regilded; one weight pulley missing.

provenance
Francis P. Garvan, New York, N.Y.

comments
Aaron Willard, Jr. succeeded to his father's business in 1823. Whether or not the younger Willard signed clocks with his name before that date is a question that has not yet been firmly answered, but it would seem logical that he probably did not, and that this clock was therefore made sometime after 1823. The scene of Aurora on the bottom glass was a popular one with ornamental painters, and appears on a clock at Winterthur (Montgomery, fig. 162) and on a clock by Zacheus Gates illustrated by Palmer (*Am. Clocks*, fig. 148). The finial on this clock is new.

The Mabel Brady Garvan Collection
1930.2631

AURORA.

glossary

ALARM ATTACHMENT. A mechanism that makes a hammer strike the bell many times. Usually the hammer is fixed on a pallet staff and is controlled by a separate weight and escape wheel.

ANCHOR-RECOIL ESCAPEMENT. See *Escapement.*

ARBOR. A rod or spindle fitted between the plates of the movement which communicates motion to other moving parts. See also *Pallet arbor.*

BRASS PLATES. See *Plates.*

BELL. That part of the clock which is struck by a hammer to indicate the time. Strictly speaking, the striking system, which includes the bell, differentiates a clock from a timepiece. The latter does not strike, but simply shows the time.

COUNT WHEEL. A wheel with a notched edge that governs the stroke of a clock in sounding the hours.

CRUTCH WIRE. A wire attached to the pallet staff to connect the pendulum. The bottom is bent at right angles for the pendulum and is known as the "crutch fork."

CUT PINION. See *Pinion.*

DEAD-BEAT ESCAPEMENT. See *Escapement.*

ESCAPEMENT. One of the essential parts of a clock, the device by which the pendulum controls the rate of timekeeping. The anchor-recoil escapement is the type of escapement usually found in ordinary clocks. It consists of an escape wheel and an oscillating anchor, or verge, with pallets, or cheeks, at each end. The anchor is fitted to an arbor called a pallet arbor, pallet staff, or verge arbor. The crutch is attached to this arbor and transmits impulses to the pendulum. The teeth of the escape wheel are released from alternate pallets of the arbor. The term "anchor-recoil" is derived from the recoil produced as the tooth on the escape wheel slides along the pallet. Opposed to this, the dead-beat escapement, invented by G. Graham ca. 1715, produces no recoil of the escape wheel when the pallet releases a tooth.

ESCAPE WHEEL. A wheel at the end of the train of wheels, engaged by the anchor whose alternate pallets receive power from it for transfer to the pendulum or other controlling elements.

LANTERN PINION. A pinion formed of two parallel heads connected by cylindrical rods or spindles spaced so that they engage the teeth of a wheel.

MOUNTING PLATE. A plate between the principal plates, those of the movement and the dial, to which the dial is often attached.

PALLET. A lip or projection to engage the teeth of a wheel.

PALLET ARBOR. The arbor to which the anchor is fitted. Sometimes called a verge arbor or pallet staff.

PENDULUM. A swinging body connected to the pallet arbor directly or by means of a crutch. It controls the rate of timekeeping, and impulses are transmitted to it by the action of the escapement. See also *Seconds pendulum.*

PILLARS. Bars of metal or wood used to establish a fixed distance between the front and back plates of the movement.

PINION. A small wheel with cogs or teeth that engage the teeth of a larger wheel. Pinions are often integral with arbors.

PLATES. Parallel pieces usually made of brass or wood into which the parts of the movement are fitted; connected at the four corners by pillars.

RACK AND SNAIL. The striking system most common in household clocks. The rack consists of an arc with ratchet teeth. This is released shortly before the hour and falls until an arm stops against the snail. The snail turns once in twelve hours and has twelve equal steps, allowing the rack to descend the number of teeth needed to strike the hour. The striking gear train then winds this back to normal position, striking one blow for each tooth that is down and then is stopped until the cycle repeats at the next hour.

SEAT BOARD. The wooden board supporting the movement; usually screwed to the pendulum case.

SECONDS PENDULUM. A pendulum that makes one oscillation per second of mean time.

TRAIN OF WHEELS. A series of wheels, or wheels and pinions, transmitting power from one to another. The wheels are usually composed of a rim, teeth, and collet (or hub) soldered to the arbor.

WEIGHTS. The weights attached by a cord or chain to the winding drum that actuate the train of wheels.

WINDING DRUM. The barrel, usually brass, onto which the cord or chain holding the weight is wound.

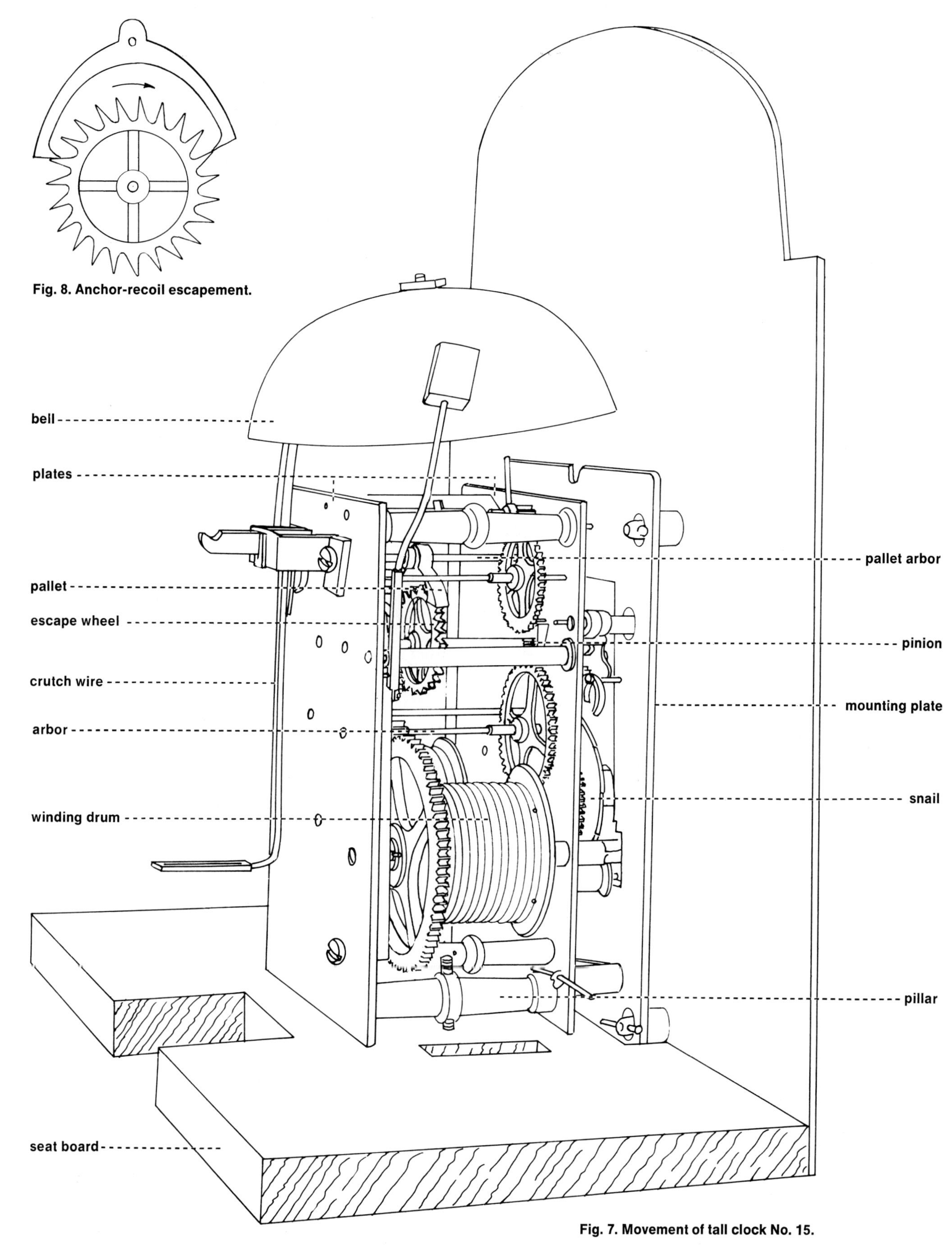

Fig. 8. Anchor-recoil escapement.

Fig. 7. Movement of tall clock No. 15.

annotated bibliography

Albright, Raymond W. *Two Centuries of Reading, Pennsylvania.* Reading: Historical Society of Berles County, 1948.

This local history of Reading contains information on the clockmaker Benjamin Witman.

Antiquarian Horology and the Proceedings of the Antiquarian Horological Society. London: The Antiquarian Horological Society.

Issued quarterly to members, this publication is generally more scholarly than its American counterpart, the *Bulletin* of the National Association of Watch and Clock Collectors, Inc.

Baillie, G. W. *Watchmakers and Clockmakers of the World.* London: Methuen & Co., Ltd., 1929.

A comprehensive list of clock- and watchmakers, without illustrations. The list is drawn from continental sources and the Minute-books of the Clockmakers Company of London, and covers the period up to 1825.

Barber, Laurence Luther. "The Clockmakers of Ashby, Massachusetts." *Antiques,* 23 (May 1933), pp. 178-180.

Barr, Lockwood Anderson. *Eli Terry Pillar and Scroll Shelf Clocks.* (n.p.) 1952.

This small pamphlet traces the development of the movements invented by Eli Terry for his wooden works clocks.

Britten, Frederick James. *Old Clocks and Watches and Their Makers: Being an Historical and Descriptive Account of the Different Styles of Clocks and Watches of the Past, in England and Abroad, to which is Added a List of Eleven Thousand Makers.* London: B. T. Batsford, 1911. Third and revised edition.

Using illustrations from the most important collections of clocks in England, the author discusses the history of English and French timekeepers. His list, the first general list of clockmakers, includes Americans.

Britten, Frederick James. *The Watch and Clockmakers' Handbook, Dictionary and Guide.* London: W. Kent & Co., and New York: E. & F.M. Spon, 1886.

A handbook with definitions of the technical terms used in watch- and clockmaking, including information useful to the young workmen and students for whom it was intended.

Bruton, Eric. *The Longcase Clock.* New York and Washington, D.C.: Frederick A. Praeger, 1968.

Tall clocks only, and for the most part the author concentrates on English examples.

Bulletin of the National Association of Watch and Clock Collectors, Inc., Columbia, Pennsylvania.

This publication, in existence since 1944, appears six times yearly, in December, February, April, June, August and October. It contains many useful articles on time-keeping devices.

Cescinsky, Herbert. *The Old English Master Clockmakers and Their Clocks 1670-1820.* New York and Toronto: Frederick A. Stokes Company, 1938.

Many illustrations of tall case and shelf clocks are included in this book, along with a helpful "Glossary of Terms Used in Clock Making."

Chase, Ada R. "Two Eighteenth-Century Clockmakers." *Antiques,* 38 (September 1940), pp. 116-118.

This article provides the best information on Reuben Ingraham and Edward Spalding.

Chase, Ada R., and Bulkeley, Houghton. "Thomas Harland's Clock—Whose Case?" *Antiques,* 87 (June 1965), pp. 700-701.

Dreppard, Carl William. *American Clocks and Clockmakers.* Boston: C.T. Branford Co., 1958. Reprinted from the 1947 edition.

In addition to photographs of tall case and nineteenth-century shelf clocks, Dreppard includes numerous reproductions of wood engravings from nineteenth-century sales catalogues. Based on the earlier lists of Mrs. Hudson Moore, Frederick Britten, and Wallace Nutting, Dreppard's list has been expanded through research in primary materials.

Drost, William E. *Clocks and Watches of New Jersey.* Elizabeth, New Jersey, 1966.

For the period 1710-1966, Drost presents biographical descriptions of New Jersey clockmakers arranged alphabetically. The volume is profusely illustrated and also contains a small section on New Jersey watchmakers.

Eckhardt, George H. *Pennsylvania Clocks and Clockmakers: An Epic of Early American Science, Industry and Craftsmanship.* New York: Devin-Adair, 1955.

This is the most complete book on Pennsylvania clocks.

Eckhardt, George H. *United States Clock and Watch Patents 1790-1890: The Record of a Century of American Horology and Enterprise.* New York: Priv. print., 1960.

Edwardes, Ernest L. *The Grandfather Clock: An Archaeological and Descriptive Essay on the Long-case Clock.* Altincham: J. Shernatt, 1952.

This was the first book to deal exclusively with the tall clock, and the text includes a number of excellent line drawings of movements and their parts.

Flynt, Henry N., and Fales, Martha Gandy. *The Heritage Foundation Collection of Silver: With Biographical Sketches of New England Silversmiths 1625-1825.* Deerfield, Massachusetts: Heritage Foundation, 1968.

Many clockmakers were also silversmiths, and the biographical sketches in this book are a useful source of information on the men who practiced both trades.

Gibbs, James W. "Early Delaware Clockmakers." *Bulletin,* National Association of Watch and Clock Collectors, 12 (February 1967), pp. 712-715.

This article is composed of short biographical sketches of twelve Delaware clockmakers.

Hering, Daniel Webster. *The Lure of the Clock: An Account of the James Arthur Collection of Clocks and Watches at New York University.* New York: The New York University Press; London: H. Milford; and Oxford: University Press, 1932.

Donated to New York University in 1925, the James Arthur collection of clocks and watches encompasses examples from all over the world. Eli and Silas Burnham Terry's clocks are discussed.

Hindle, Brooke. *David Rittenhouse.* Princeton, New Jersey: Princeton University Press, 1964.

This thorough biography of the life and work of one of America's leading eighteenth-century scientists unfortunately is not illustrated with many of his clocks.

Hoopes, Penrose R. *Connecticut Clockmakers of the Eighteenth Century.* Hartford, Connecticut: E. V. Mitchell, and New York: Dodd, Mead & Company, 1930.

After brief introductory chapters on the history of Connecticut clockmaking, this book contains biographical sketches on seventy-nine clockmakers and sixty-six illustrations of clocks.

Hoopes, Penrose Robinson. *Shop Records of Daniel Burnap, Clockmaker.* Hartford, Connecticut: Connecticut Historical Society, 1958.

From the shop records, account books, and tools of Daniel Burnap, deposited at the Connecticut Historical Society, Penrose Hoopes has written a study of the life of this East Windsor, Connecticut, clockmaker, instrument maker, silversmith, and brass founder in the years following the American Revolution.

Hoopes, Penrose R. "Some Minor Connecticut Clockmakers." *Antiques,* 27 (September 1935), pp. 104-105.

Seven more names are added to Hoopes's definitive list of Connecticut clockmakers published in *Connecticut Clockmakers of the Eighteenth Century.*

Hummel, Charles F. *With Hammer in Hand: The Dominy Craftsmen of East Hampton, L. I., New York.* Charlottesville, Virginia: The University of Virginia Press, 1968.

This family of East Hampton, L. I., craftsmen were clockmakers as well as cabinetmakers. A number of their clocks have survived and are illustrated and discussed here along with their clockmaking tools.

James, Arthur E. *Chester County Clocks and Their Makers.* West Chester, Pennsylvania: Chester County Historical Society, 1947.

This volume includes fifty-three sketches on clockmakers, with much of the information drawn from primary sources.

Jerome, Chauncey. *History of the American Clock Business for the Past Sixty Years, and Life of Chauncey Jerome.* New Haven: F. C. Dayton, Jr., 1860.

As the first autobiography of an American craftsman and businessman, Jerome's book is as important for the insights into his attitudes about himself as it is for information on the early years of the industrialization of clockmaking.

MacQuoid, Percy, and Edwards, Ralph. *The Dictionary of English Furniture.* 3 vols. London: Country Life, and New York: Charles Scribner's Sons, 1924.

Maust, Don. *Early American Clocks: A Collection of Essays on Early American Clocks and Their Makers.* Uniontown, Pennsylvania: E. G. Warman Pub. Co., 1971.

These valuable little essays give detailed information on a number of clockmakers, many of whom worked in the nineteenth century.

Montgomery, Charles F. *American Furniture: The Federal Period in the Henry Francis duPont Winterthur Museum.* New York: The Viking Press. 1966.

This catalogue of the Federal style furniture at the Winterthur Museum discusses seven tall and dwarf tall clocks, and more than twenty wall and shelf clocks.

Moore, Mrs. Hannah (Hudson). *The Old Clock Book.* New York: Frederick A. Stokes Co., 1911.

Mrs. Moore discusses both English and American clocks and watches. A list of English clockmakers, drawn from the Books of the Clockmakers' Company in London; the first workable list of American clockmakers has a prominent place at the end of the book.

Nelson, William, ed. *Documents Relating to the Colonial History of the State of New Jersey. First Series: Extracts from American Newspapers Relating to New Jersey 1768-1769.* Vol. VII. Patterson, New Jersey, 1894-1923.

New England Clocks at Old Sturbridge Village: The J. Cheney Welles Collection. Sturbridge, Massachusetts: 1955.

Nutting, Wallace. *The Clock Book.* Framingham, Massachusetts: Old America Company, 1924.

Nutting includes in this volume over 250 photographs, a list of foreign makers (taken from Frederick Britten), and a list of American makers (expanded from Hannah Moore).

Nutting, Wallace. *Furniture Treasury.* 3 vols. Framingham, Massachusetts: Old America Company, 1933.

The material from *The Clock Book* is enlarged in the three volumes of the *Furniture Treasury.* The list of makers at the end of Vol. III doubles the earlier list.

Palmer, Brooks. *The Book of American Clocks.* New York: MacMillan, 1959.

Composed of a brief introduction, followed by over three hundred illustrations and a list of American clockmakers that includes more than six thousand names.

Palmer, Brooks. *A Treasury of American Clocks.* New York and London: The MacMillan Company, 1967.

As a companion and sequel to *The Book of American Clocks,* this volume contains 550 photographs not included in its predecessor and additional names and information in the list of clockmakers.

Prime, Alfred Coxe. *The Arts and Crafts in Philadelphia, Maryland and South Carolina 1786-1800.* Series II, The Walpole Society, 1932.

A chapter containing clock- and watchmakers' advertisements is included in this volume.

Randall, Richard Jr. *American Furniture in the Museum of Fine Arts, Boston.* Boston: Museum of Fine Arts, 1965.

This catalogue of the American furniture in the Museum of Fine Arts discusses more than a dozen clocks.

Rice, Norman S. *New York Furniture Before 1840 in the Collection of the Albany Institute of History and Art.* The Albany Institute of History and Art, 1962.

Rice, Norman S. and Halpin, James H. "Joseph Warford, Silversmith of Albany and Salem, New York." *Antiques,* 85 (April 1964), pp. 429-430.

The silversmith and clockmaker Joseph Warford was in partnership with Nehemiah Basset. Their tall clock is included here as No. 22.

Roberts, Kenneth D. *Some Observations Concerning Connecticut Clockmaking, 1790-1850.* A Supplement to the *Bulletin* of the National Association of Watch and Clock Collectors, Inc. No. 6 of a Series. Columbia, Pennsylvania, Summer 1970.

This publication is relatively brief (43 pages), but it admirably covers a crucial period in the Connecticut clock industry. The author makes considerable use of primary materials.

Sketch, Carolyn Wood. "Early Colonial Clockmakers in Philadelphia." *Pennsylvania Magazine of History and Biography,* 56 (1932), pp. 225-235.

The author discusses the Philadelphia clockmakers Peter and Thomas Sketch, Owen Biddle, and John Wood, Jr.

Willard, John Ware. *A History of Simon Willard, Inventor and Clockmaker.* Boston: E. O. Cockayne, Printer, 1911.

This is undoubtedly the first detailed study of an American craftsman. The author, the great-grandson of this famous American clockmaker, illustrated the volume profusely and included other clockmakers from the Willard circle.

index